# The Ties that Divide:
## History, Honour and Territory in Sino-Japanese Relations

William Choong

# The Ties that Divide:
## History, Honour and Territory in Sino-Japanese Relations

William Choong

IISS The International Institute for Strategic Studies

# The International Institute for Strategic Studies

Arundel House | 13–15 Arundel Street | Temple Place | London | WC2R 3DX | UK

First published October 2014 by **Routledge**
4 Park Square, Milton Park, Abingdon, Oxon, OX14 4RN

for **The International Institute for Strategic Studies**
Arundel House, 13–15 Arundel Street, Temple Place, London, WC2R 3DX, UK
www.iiss.org

Simultaneously published in the USA and Canada by **Routledge**
270 Madison Ave., New York, NY 10016

*Routledge is an imprint of Taylor & Francis, an Informa Business*

© 2014 The International Institute for Strategic Studies

DIRECTOR-GENERAL AND CHIEF EXECUTIVE Dr John Chipman
EDITOR Dr Nicholas Redman
COPY EDITOR Dr Jeffrey Mazo
EDITORIAL Jill Lally
COVER/PRODUCTION John Buck, Kelly Verity
COVER IMAGES Asahi Shimbun/Getty; Jean S. and Frederic A. Sharf Collection at
the Museum of Fine Arts, Boston

**The International Institute for Strategic Studies** is an independent centre for research, information and debate on the problems of conflict, however caused, that have, or potentially have, an important military content. The Council and Staff of the Institute are international and its membership is drawn from almost 100 countries. The Institute is independent and it alone decides what activities to conduct. It owes no allegiance to any government, any group of governments or any political or other organisation. The IISS stresses rigorous research with a forward-looking policy orientation and places particular emphasis on bringing new perspectives to the strategic debate.

The Institute's publications are designed to meet the needs of a wider audience than its own membership and are available on subscription, by mail order and in good book-shops. Further details at www.iiss.org.

Printed and bound in Great Britain by Bell & Bain Ltd, Thornliebank, Glasgow

British Library Cataloguing in Publication Data
A catalogue record for this book is available from the British Library

Library of Congress Cataloging in Publication Data

ADELPHI series
ISSN 1944-5571

ADELPHI 445
ISBN 978-1-138-88565-3

# Contents

ACKNOWLEDGEMENTS

This book project started when I was a journalist at the Singapore *Straits Times*. From my front-row seat, I realised that there was a combustible mix at work in the Sino-Japanese relationship. While the controversial history of the two countries was the fuel, the dispute over the Senkaku/Diaoyu Islands was the spark. This Adelphi is the result.

I want to thank the scholars and analysts who, over a cup of coffee, ramen or *jiaozi*, have shared their inputs and insights with me. They include Mou Hong, Yuichi Hosoya, Hu Hao, Hu Jiping, Li Quoqiang, Liu Jiangyong, Eiichi Katahara, Yasuhiro Matsuda, Narushige Michishita, Cen Song, Akio Takahara, Cao Qun, Wang Dong and Wang Xiaowei. A note of special thanks should go to Stephanie Kleine-Ahlbrandt, who regaled me with tales of Sino-Japanese amity and animosity over a bowl of laksa (fiery recipe for a fiery tale). Hitoshi Tanaka, with his depth of experience at the Japanese Ministry of Foreign Affairs, was particularly helpful in providing me with a sage introduction into the subject. I also want to thank my former *Straits Times* colleagues – Kor Kian Beng, Ho Ai Li and Kwan Weng Kin – for opening up their rolodexes prior to my research trip, topped up with the friendly exchange of notes and anecdotes that so marks the tradecraft of journalism. Several officials from various capitals provided critical inputs. For reasons outlined in the first paragraph, they will remain anonymous.

At the IISS, I want to thank the gang at the Asia office – Tim Huxley, Alex Neill, Hanna Ucko-Neill, Pierre Noël, Clara Lee, Eva Saddiqui, Katherine Scully and Michelle Chin – for their useful input and understanding when I spent hours holed up in my usual space. A special word of thanks also goes to my colleagues in London – Christian Le Mière, Henry Boyd and James Hackett – for going through the trickier military parts of the manuscript. This work would not have been complete (or have reached completion) without the professional handling of editors Nick Redman and Jeffrey Mazo and Design Manager John Buck.

Last but not least, I would like to thank my wife Lay Fong and sons Joseph and Jonathan, whose prayers ('Jesus, please help daddy finish his *Adelphi* – soon!') propelled the project (and associated writer) to the finish line.

# GLOSSARY

| | |
|---|---|
| **A2/AD** | Anti-access/area-denial |
| **ADIZ** | Air Defence Identification Zone |
| **ADMM-Plus** | ASEAN Defence Ministers' Meeting Plus |
| **APEC** | Asia-Pacific Economic Cooperation |
| **ARF** | ASEAN Regional Forum |
| **ASCM** | Anti-ship cruise missile |
| **ASEAN** | Association of Southeast Asian Nations |
| **ASM** | Anti-ship missile |
| **ASW** | Anti-submarine warfare |
| **BCE** | Before the Common Era |
| **CCP** | Chinese Communist Party |
| **CE** | Common Era |
| **CMS** | China Marine Surveillance |
| **CUES** | Code for Unplanned Encounters at Sea |
| **DPJ** | Democratic Party of Japan |
| **EAC** | East Asian Community |
| **EAS** | East Asia Summit |
| **ECAFE** | Economic Commission for Asia and the Far East |
| **EEZ** | Exclusive economic zone |
| **FDI** | Foreign direct investment |
| **G2** | Group of 2 |
| **HADR** | Humanitarian assistance and disaster relief |
| **ICJ** | International Court of Justice |
| **ISR** | Intelligence, surveillance and reconnaissance |
| **JASDF** | Japan Air Self Defense Force |

| | |
|---|---|
| **JCG** | Japan Coast Guard |
| **JCMCM** | Japan–China Maritime Communications Mechanism |
| **JMSDF** | Japan Maritime Self Defense Force |
| **JSDF** | Japan Self Defense Force |
| **LDP** | Liberal Democratic Party |
| **NDPG** | National Defense Program Guidelines |
| **NIDS** | National Institute of Defense Studies |
| **ODA** | Official Development Assistance |
| **PLA** | People's Liberation Army |
| **PLAAF** | People's Liberation Army Air Force |
| **PLAN** | People's Liberation Army Navy |
| **PRC** | People's Republic of China |
| **ROC** | Republic of China |
| **SAR** | Search and rescue |
| **SRBM** | Short-range ballistic missile |
| **UNCLOS** | United Nations Convention on the Law of the Sea |
| **WPNS** | Western Pacific Naval Symposium |

# EVENTS AT A GLANCE

| | |
|---|---|
| **1621** | According to Beijing, a map produced under the Ming Dynasty indicates the Diaoyu Islands as part of China's maritime territory. |
| **January 1895** | The Japanese government formally obtains control of the Diaoyu (Senkaku) Islands. Japan asserts the islands were not owned by anyone prior to their occupation. |
| **September 1945** | The islands, as part of Ryukyu Islands, come under US government control after the surrender of Japan at the end of the Second World War. |
| **June 1951** | In a memo prepared by US Secretary of State John Foster Dulles for a meeting with Secretary of Defense George Marshall, Dulles remarked that the US did not want sovereignty over the islands. Dulles observed that the United States could only receive a grant of exclusive administrative, legislative and jurisdiction rights as long as Japan was sovereign. He wrote that 'exclusive strategic control is entirely compatible with residual sovereignty elsewhere, provided the sovereign grants it'. |
| **September 1951** | The Treaty of San Francisco, which officially ends the occupation of Japan by the victorious powers and returns sovereignty to Japan, does not mention the Senkaku Islands. Like Okinawa, the Senkaku Islands are initially administered in trust by the US. The United States pays rent to a private owner, as it uses the islands for target practice for bombers. The Japanese view this as an implicit US recognition of Japanese sovereignty over the islands. |
| **May 1969** | The United Nations Economic Commission for Asia and the Far East discovers potential oil and gas reserves in the vicinity of the Diaoyu/Senkaku Islands. |
| **June 1971** | The Agreement between Japan and the United States of America Concerning the Ryukyu Islands and the Daito Islands is signed between Japan and the US, returning the Senkaku Islands (as part of the Ryukyu Islands) to Japanese administration. This triggers the first anti-Japanese protests, led by Taiwan. |
| **August 1978** | The Japan–China Peace and Friendship Treaty is signed between China and Japan, in which the dispute over the islands is put aside for future resolution. |
| **October 1978** | China's Deng Xiaoping proposes shelving the dispute over the Diaoyu/Senkaku Islands in favour of furthering bilateral relations during his visit to Japan. |

| | |
|---|---|
| **February 1992** | The National People's Congress in China passes a resolution affirming Chinese sovereignty over the Diaoyu Islands. |
| **September 1996** | A Hong Kong activist drowns after jumping into waters off the Diaoyu Islands during a pro-China protest. |
| **March 2004** | Activist Feng Jinhua and six others from China land on the Diaoyu Islands, the first time mainland activists successfully land on the islands. |
| **November 2004** | A Chinese *Han*-class nuclear attack submarine travels submerged through the Ishigaki Strait. |
| **June 2008** | China and Japan agree to jointly develop four gas fields in the East China Sea while halting development in other contested parts of the region. |
| **November 2008** | Four Chinese warships, including a *Luzhou*-class destroyer, pass through the Miyako Strait on the way to the Pacific Ocean. |
| **June 2009** | A *Luzhou*-class destroyer and four other vessels traverse the Miyako Strait. |
| **March 2010** | Six warships, including a *Luzhou*-class destroyer, pass through the Miyako Strait to the Pacific Ocean. |
| **April 2010** | Ten warships and two submarines pass through the Miyako Strait; a Chinese helicopter buzzes a JMSDF escort ship. |
| **July 2010** | Two vessels, including a *Luzhou*-class destroyer, pass through the Miyako Strait. |
| **March 2011** | A PLA Y-8 patrol aircraft and a Y-8 intelligence-gathering aircraft cross the Japan–China median line and approach within approximately 50km of Japan's airspace near the Senkaku/Diaoyu Islands. |
| **June 2011** | Eleven Chinese vessels, including three *Sovremenny*-class destroyers, transit the Miyako Strait. |
| **April 2012** | During his visit to Washington DC, Tokyo Governor Shintaro Ishihara publicly states his desire for Tokyo to purchase the Diaoyu/Senkaku Islands from their private owner. |
| **July 2012** | Prime Minister Yoshihiko Noda announces the Japanese government's plan to purchase the islands. |
| **September 2012** | On 10 September Japan completes the purchase of the islands. Tokyo says the purchase from a private Japanese owner represents an effort aimed at diffusing territorial tensions. On 15 September the biggest anti-Japanese protests since China and Japan normalised diplomatic relations in 1972 are held in cities across China. The Japanese embassy in Beijing is besieged by thousands of protesters throwing rocks, eggs and bottles. On 18 September two Japanese activists land on the Senkaku/Diaoyu Islands while widespread anti-Japanese protests are held across China at the anniversary of Japan's invasion of Manchuria. |
| **October 2012** | Seven PLAN vessels transit the Miyako Strait to the Pacific Ocean. On 17 October the same seven vessels – destroyers, frigates, a refuelling vessel and a submarine-rescue vessel – transit back to the East China Sea through the Taiwan–Yonaguni Strait. |
| **November 2012** | Five vessels – two guided-missile destroyers, two missile frigates and a supply ship – pass through the Miyako Strait on their way to the Pacific Ocean to conduct training exercises. |

| | |
|---|---|
| December 2012 | A Chinese surveillance aircraft enters the airspace over the Senkaku Islands. According to Japanese statements, this is the first such incident since 1958. Japan sends eight F-15 fighters. |
| January 2013 | On 19 January a *Jiangkai* I-class frigate is suspected to have locked its fire-control radar on a helicopter based on a JMSDF destroyer in the East China Sea. On 30 January a *Jiangwei* II-class frigate allegedly directs its fire-control radar at a JMSDF destroyer. |
| February 2013 | Japan lodges a protest over the second radar lock-on incident. |
| November 2013 | China announces the establishment of an ADIZ in the East China Sea that overlaps with Japan's own ADIZ. China's ADIZ includes the disputed islands. The US sends a pair of B-52 bombers into China's newly established ADIZ. The US deliberately violates rules set by China by refusing to inform Beijing about the flight, officials say. |
| January 2014 | Japan scrambles fighter jets to head off a Chinese government plane flying towards the Senkaku/Diaoyus. This is the first incident to be announced by Japan's Defence Ministry after China's declaration of an ADIZ in the East China Sea. |
| March 2014 | Japanese Foreign Minister Fumio Kishida urges China to establish a maritime defence communication mechanism, which has already been agreed to in principle. |
| April 2014 | US President Barack Obama states that Washington is obliged to defend the Senkaku Islands, but urges both China and Japan to resolve their territorial dispute peacefully. |
| August 2014 | Chinese coast-guard ships sail into the territorial waters of the Senkaku/Diaoyu Islands, after Tokyo's latest annual defence paper warns of China's 'dangerous acts' near the disputed archipelago. |
| September 2014 | Japanese Deputy Foreign Minister Shinsuke Sugiyama tells reporters he met Chinese counterpart Vice Foreign Minister Liu Zhenmin. The two men discussed the possibility of holding summits between their leaders amid strained ties over territorial and historical issues. |

INTRODUCTION

China and Japan share deep historical, cultural and linguistic roots. In 1992, Chinese General Secretary Jiang Zemin declared that the two peoples, separated by a narrow strip of water, had forged a 'profound relationship through their exchanges for more than two thousand years'.[1] His speech marked a high point in relations between the countries, which had reaped the benefits of trade, foreign investment and people-to-people exchanges sown in the normalisation of relations 20 years previously.

Twenty years later, despite a deepening of commercial and financial ties, bilateral relations were antagonistic. In September 2012, Japan 'nationalised' three islands in the Senkaku chain, known to China (which also claims them) as the Diaoyus.[2] The decision led to demonstrations across China; in Beijing, protesters pelted the Japanese Embassy with eggs and paint. In January 2013, Japan alleged that Chinese naval vessels operating in the vicinity of the islands had twice locked their fire-control radars on Japanese counterparts. In response to what it deemed to be increased Chinese incursions into Japanese territorial waters around the islands, Tokyo issued a Defense White Paper exhibiting strong antipathy towards Beijing. A thousand Japanese troops took part in the US military's annual *Operation Dawn Blitz*, an amphibious exercise simulating an assault on an island to recapture territory in the face of enemy fire. Nor was China lacking in the rhetorical stakes. The People's Liberation Army (PLA) released a military-themed video game, *Glorious Mission*, which included an update giving players the chance to fight for the disputed islands. Japanese attempts to convene a high-level summit with China failed, and traditional backchannels for diplomacy between Beijing and Tokyo closed.

It could be argued that a host of contemporary problems led China and Japan to this low point in relations – the enduring strength of the US–Japan alliance; Tokyo's post-2001 efforts towards remilitarisation; its shift to the right during Shinzo Abe's second term as prime minister; and Beijing's perception that the US sought to contain its 'peaceful rise' through a network of alliances and partnerships across the Asia-Pacific. These tensions have trumped the economic interdependency created by sustained trade, investment and commercial linkages going back decades.

But a focus solely on contemporary issues misses the fact that bilateral relations between Japan and China have always been cyclical, turning from conflict to cooperation and back again. In 1874, Li Hongzhang, minister for foreign affairs for China's last imperial dynasty, wrote to his emperor that Japan was at China's courtyard gates and intruding into its emptiness and solitude; in time, Japan would become 'China's permanent and great anxiety'.[3] Li qualified his pessimistic prognosis by forecasting – correctly – that over the next 50 years Sino-Japanese relations would see recurring cycles of confrontation and cooperation.[4] Between 1894 and 1945, Japan's military forces overran China's main industrial areas and killed millions of Chinese, a deep wound that is still felt. After the end of the Pacific War, the two states maintained peaceable if distant relations until 1972, when diplomatic ties were normalised. That created a platform for stability in Northeast Asia and the flourishing relationship hailed by Jiang in 1992. It also echoed a point made by Li to his Japanese counterpart in 1895: that China and Japan's natural affinities would help to maintain the general stability of Asia, such that the 'Asiatic yellow race will not be encroached upon by the white race of Europe'.[5]

By the late twentieth century, however, bilateral relations had taken a turn for the worse, as deep-seated animosities began to reassert themselves. In China, sentiment towards Japan reverted to a 'historically rooted and visceral distrust' that was largely a consequence of Japanese atrocities in China in the 1930s.[6] In Japan, by contrast, there was disquiet at China's growing economic strength and its increased assertiveness globally, which seemed to signal that Beijing was on the way to becoming a great power once more. Japanese wariness of China's geopolitical ambitions was such that, by December 2010 when its National Defense Program Guidelines for FY2011 were published, the government had begun to revise its defence posture dramatically. According to the document, the Japan Self Defense Force (JSDF) was to move from a relatively static posture of positioning tanks in the northern island of Hokkaido to a more dynamic posture based on intelligence, surveillance and reconnaissance (ISR), maritime patrol and air defence. The JSDF would also strengthen ballistic-missile defence capabilities, including in the country's southwestern islands.[7] In September 2013, Shinzo Abe, Japan's right-leaning prime minister, borrowed the oft-used imagery of Korea as a dagger pointed at the heart of Japan to describe Sino-Japanese relations. In his view, China was a 'strategic dagger' pointed at Japan.[8]

Three factors should be noted when considering the poor current state of bilateral relations. Firstly, the cool-headed decision of national leaders in the 1970s to shelve contentious issues such as Japan's wartime record and the question of sovereignty over the Senkaku/Diaoyu Islands has been overturned. In its place, both sides are indulging in nationalism and an inclination toward irrational or risky behaviour. Secondly, China and Japan have invested much more in their claims to the islands than is justified by their value or the costs of an open conflict over them. Thirdly, neither the cultural and linguistic affinities between the two countries nor their economic interdependence preclude the possibility of such a conflict. Scholars on both sides of the East China Sea are concerned that hostilities could escalate and even lead to war.[9]

Disputes over historiography and the Senkakus/Diaoyus, coupled with an increased focus on the part of both navies towards the East China Sea, have increased the likelihood of military conflict in a region of vital importance to the global economy. For more than 40 years, China and Japan have been largely successful in developing relations with countries in the Asia-Pacific (in particular the members of the Association of Southeast Asian Nations (ASEAN)), contributing to regional security. Open conflict between the two states would eradicate decades of goodwill built up after 1972. It would cut off people-to-people exchanges between China and Japan and endanger the sea lanes so crucial for global commerce and supply-chain networks.

For China, a war with Japan over the disputed islands would scupper all its claims of a 'peaceful rise' and its desire for a stable regional environment to support its drive for economic growth and modernisation. The toll would be heavy for Japan too. The modest economic growth achieved by Abenomics – a mix of monetary easing, infrastructure spending and a focus on structural reforms in the Japanese economy – could be thrown into reverse and, more importantly, Japan's carefully cultivated image as a pacifist country that has disavowed force would be ruined.

Moreover, a bilateral dispute would quickly become a regional one. The US, long the guarantor of Asian security and ally of Japan, would be compelled to come to Tokyo's aid. Even if Washington were to do so in a manner designed to limit the fallout for its own ties with China, the consequences for Sino-American relations would be immense. Furthermore, Asian countries might have to take a decision they have so far managed to avoid: picking sides between the US and China.

Changes in Asia's regional security architecture, such as the emergence of a Group of 2 (G2) between China and the United States, or a concert of Asia underpinned by multilateral institutions such as the East Asia Summit (EAS) and the ASEAN Defence Minister's Meetings Plus (ADMM-Plus), might have a positive effect on the Sino-Japanese relationship, but it would take time. There is a pressing need for China and Japan to work out mutually acceptable arrangements to prevent a further deterioration in relations. Identifying such steps requires understanding their disputes over historiography and territory, and how these are affected by their military postures, the US-Japanese alliance and the regional security architecture.

## Notes

[1] Caroline Rose, *Interpreting History in Sino-Japanese Relations: A Case Study in Political Decision-Making* (London: Routledge, 1998), p. 5.

[2] In this Adelphi I will refer to the chain as the 'Senkaku/Diaoyu Islands', except where discussing individual national territorial claims, when I use the relevant national nomenclature.

[3] Cited in Allen S. Whiting, *China Eyes Japan* (Berkeley, CA: University of California Press, 1989), p. 27.

[4] *Ibid.*, p. 30.

[5] *Ibid.*, p. 27.

[6] Thomas J. Christensen, 'China, the U.S.–Japan Alliance and the Security Dilemma in East Asia',

*International Security*, vol. 23, no. 4, Spring 1999, p. 52.

7   See 'National Defense Program Guidelines for FY2011 and Beyond', Japan Ministry of Defense, 17 December 2010, p. 13, at http://www.mod.go.jp/e/d_act/d_policy/pdf/guidelinesFY2011.pdf, and Eric Sayers, 'The "Consequent Interest" of Japan's Southwestern Islands: A Mahanian Appraisal of the Ryukyu Archipelago', *Naval War College Review*, vol. 66, no. 2, Spring 2013, pp. 45–61.

8   Joel Assogba, 'Stand Up to Abe for the Sake of Japan, Asia's Future', *Japan Times*, 30 April 2013.

9   Interviews in Beijing and Tokyo, August and September 2013.

# CHAPTER ONE

# The historical context

For Japan, from prehistory to relatively recent times, the outside world *was* China. Relations with their mammoth continental neighbour was the most pressing foreign-policy issue for Japanese decision-makers. During these centuries of interaction there were many periods which saw strong and mutually beneficial relations between the two societies. The common Japanese phrase *dobun doshu* ('same script, same race') describes Japan's cultural debt to China. Japan adopted the Chinese writing system, borrowed China's more advanced technology and emulated China's political institutions.[1]

Moreover, despite the asymmetry in size between the two powers, there were periods when China was positively influenced by Japan. Japan's modernisation during the Meiji Restoration was seen by many Chinese intellectuals as a model for emulation. Many Chinese spent their formative years studying in Japan, while Japanese scholars created much of China's modern lexicography, drawing on classical Chinese in the same way that Western scholars drew on Greek and Latin in the eighteenth and nineteenth centuries.

## Two millennia of relations

Interactions between China and Japan were recorded in the time of China's Qin (221–207 BCE) and Han (206 BCE–220 CE) dynasties, particularly following the incorporation of Korea into China's empire in 108 BCE.[2] Some four hundred years later, the northern Kyushu state of Yamatai was ruled by a queen who maintained relations with the Wei Kingdom in China, one of the three states that emerged from the ashes of the Han Empire. The Yamatai queen was presented with the seal of 'monarch of the Wo' ('small' or 'pygmy', the Chinese term for Japan, the Japanese people being referred to as *wo-jen* and the nation *wo-kuo*). This presumption of China's superiority has continued through the centuries.

Between the fifth and tenth centuries the relationship blossomed; Chinese social, cultural, economic and political influence on Japan during this period is evident. Institutions developed under China's Sui (581–618 CE) and Tang (618–907 CE) dynasties served as models for Japan. Most significant among these were the introduction of Buddhism and Confucianism, the adaptation of the Chinese writing system, and Chinese arts and crafts. These influences, in addition to economic and political borrowings, helped to transform Japan. Under the leadership of Shotoku Taishi, Japan adopted a 17-article constitution laying down the fundamental precepts relating to the maintenance of the state and the observance of Confucian morality. It also stressed a respect for harmony, the study of Buddhism and obedience to the emperor. Buddhism and Confucianism became the hallmarks of the 'Asuka culture', as Asuka became the imperial capital of Japan.

In 663 CE, during the Tang period, there was a war between two rival Korean kingdoms, Silla and Paekche, in which China fought alongside the former. Paekche requested Japanese aid after being attacked by Silla and Tang forces. Japan sent supplies and troops to Korea, but the empress died while directing operations and the combined Tang and Silla forces subsequently routed Japanese forces at the mouth of the Kim River. The defeat prompted Japan to withdraw from the peninsula and enter a period of self-imposed isolation. It was only in 710 that relations with Tang China were fully resumed. Japan adopted many of the achievements of Tang culture but, to a greater degree than during the Asuka period, adapted them to suit local tastes and traditions. This included an emphasis on Buddhism as the political system, based on the Ritsuryo Code that drew from the Confucian teachings of China.

Between the seventh and ninth centuries, at least 14 major Japanese delegations made the difficult journey across the East China Sea. They brought back knowledge, skills and goods that would affect every aspect of Japanese life. The expeditions included not only diplomats and priests but carpenters, doctors, engineers, gardeners, historians, metalworkers, musicians and translators. Enthusiasm for and interest in China was so great that some delegations, members of which could run into the hundreds, would stay years or even decades to complete their studies.[3] In 804, for example, a 30-year-old monk named Kukai set sail for China as part of a Japanese government delegation and made his way to the capital Chang-an (present-day Xian), one of the world's most prosperous cities at the time. Over the next two years Kukai studied Buddhism and Sanskrit, excelled at the Chinese writing system, and observed first-hand the achievements of science and engineering of Tang China. The voyage transformed Kukai into one of Japan's most influential figures. He established the Shingon ('True Word') Buddhist school, worked on refining and spreading the Japanese syllabary, founded the first private school for commoners and instructed his compatriots on temple construction and public works projects.[4]

During the Tang period and thereafter, Chinese influence over Japan was a function of the strength of the Chinese state. Beginning in the middle of the ninth century, Japan began to distance itself from China's political system. In 858 Japan moved beyond the Confucian system in the Kyoto court with the introduction of a shogun. In the eleventh century it distanced itself further, with the emergence of the first provincial samurai. By this time the Tang dynasty had fallen, and Chinese influence had dissipated. Thus the Tendai and Shingon sects began to 'Japanise' Buddhism to give it a stronger Japanese character. Despite this cultural distancing by Japan, however, economic interaction remained high. During China's Song Dynasty (960–1279), between 40 and 50 trading vessels plied the waters between the two countries every year.

In the late thirteenth century the two nations clashed again. By the time of the Mongol Yuan Dynasty founded by Kublai Khan (1271–1368), Japanese pirates known as *wako* (Chinese *wokou*) threatened the Chinese coast and China responded with attempted attacks on the Japanese islands. China sent envoys to Japan with a demand for tribute, which the Japanese regent, Hojo Tokimune, rejected outright. In 1274 and 1281 the Mongols send a large number of vessels to invade northern Kyushu. Japan was saved by a combination of its samurai and storms (*kamikaze* or 'divine winds') that decimated the Mongol forces. One consequence of this escape was the emergence of a belief in Japan's 'divinity powers and splendid isolation' – a mindset that permeated the Japanese psyche up to the Second World War.[5] The abortive Mongol attack also led to further Japanisation, as the samurai class gained political power and indigenous Japanese culture took root. This effectively wiped out any vestiges of Tang culture.

In the fourteenth century, the powerful Ming Dynasty (1368–1644) forced Japan into a tributary relationship. Japan grudgingly accepted its inferior status until 1547, when it stopped paying tribute and began to compete with China for control of the Korean Peninsula. It was during the Ming Dynasty that the first economic and commercial ties between Japan and China were formally established. Japanese commercial culture developed tremendously and Chinese copper coins circulated widely in Japan. The monetisation of the Japanese economy also took off thanks to Chinese inputs. Twice, in 1592 and 1597, the two states came to blows over Japan's attempts to expand into Korea. Japan, emboldened by its newfound trading prowess, which was founded on trading silver in Formosa, Annam, Siam and Southeast Asia, asked Korea to act as an intermediary to force Ming China to pay tribute to Japan. Both campaigns ultimately failed and, after the death of the regent Hideyoshi Toyotomi in 1598, Japan withdrew its troops from Korea. These military campaigns reflected the rise of militaristic elements in Japan and the country's aspiration to assert itself against its much larger neighbour.

Thereafter Japan retreated into isolation (*sakoku*) for two centuries under the Tokugawa Shogunate (1600–1868), which saw government by the warrior class. Foreign influences on Japan's political and cultural life were mostly eradicated. Following the demise of the Ming in China, the new Manchu Qing Dynasty (1644–1911) made no effort to resume official relations with Japan or attempt to draw Japan into the tributary system. Japan's isolationist policy put strict limits on official trade relations, but a robust unofficial network operated across Asia, ranging from the Persian Gulf in the west to Mexico's Acapulco Bay in the east. Sino-Japanese economic ties were largely mediated by third parties, most significantly Taiwan, the Ryukyus and Korea. The contrast between political and commercial ties was striking, and resembled in some ways the 'hot economics, cold politics' relations that characterise interactions between China and Japan in the early twenty-first century.

## The modern period

*Western encroachment and the Meiji Restoration*

US Commodore Matthew Perry struck the death knell for Japan's policy of isolation when in 1853 he entered Uraga harbour at the entrance to Tokyo Bay with a squadron of four warships and sought to force Japan to trade openly with the US. The following year, he obtained an agreement whereby two ports, Shimoda and Hakodate, would be opened to US ships for fuel, water and food. Japan signed similar treaties with Britain, Russia, Holland and France. These trade treaties, as well as the shelling of Shimonoseki by the combined naval forces of the US, Britain, France and the Netherlands in 1864, dealt a politically devastating blow to the Tokugawa system. There were demands for the end of the shogunate and return to direct imperial rule, to assert Japan's independence and minimise foreign interference. In 1868 power was formally transferred from the shogun to Emperor Meiji, who had taken the throne the previous year.

The Meiji Restoration (1853–1894), which saw Japan emerge as a modern state by the early twentieth century through intensive Westernisation and industrialisation, altered the nature of Japanese–Chinese relations. In a reversal of the historical pattern in which China was the stronger power, able to exert influence on Japan, in the late 1800s Japan was a rising power while China under the Manchu Qing Dynasty was in decline.

Meiji-era Japan drew heavily on Western expertise, particularly in the military arena. From 1868, Japan's army and navy benefited from, and contributed to, modernisation in other sectors of society. Conscription was introduced in the early 1870s and a centralised system of military education saw officers sent abroad to study. In 1878, an independent general staff was created, followed in 1883 by a staff college.[6] Foreign advisers, including the Englishman John Ingles and the German Jacob Meckel, did much to bring Japan's military to a high state of efficiency. Meckel helped to reorganise the war ministry, refine the general staff, and develop military education, logistics and medical services.[7]

As Japan adopted the technology of more advanced Western powers, it sought also to replicate their imperial inclinations. As many parts of the world fell under the control of Western powers, as historian John Dower put it, Japan 'emulated them and joined their banquet'.[8] In 1874, Japan sent a punative expeditionary force to Formosa (Taiwan), then nominally under Qing suzerainty. In 1876, Japan employed gunboat diplomacy to coerce Korea into signing the Kanghwa Treaty, which opened up Korean ports to Japanese ships and detached Korea from its tributary relationship with China.

*Historical enmity (1895–1945)*

The half-century between 1895 and 1945 was marked by conflicts between China and Japan that left an indelible wound in the Chinese national psyche (see Map 1). In 1894–95 the two countries clashed over Korea, a vassal state of China since the seventeenth century. After a series of Japanese victories in Korea, Manchuria and China and at sea, the Qing government signed the Treaty of Shimonoseki on 17 April 1895, recognising Korean independence and ceding it as a tributary nation. Defeat at the hands of the 'eastern barbarians' was a huge shock for China and signalled the beginning of the end for the Qing Dynasty. The treaty also gave Japan control of Taiwan and the Pescadore Islands in the Taiwan Strait. The 1894–95 Sino-Japanese conflict reflects a common dynamic in international affairs in which one injustice leads to another. Japan, having suffered coercion and exploitation at the hands of the US Navy in 1853, inflicted very much the same on China in 1894.

The First World War proved another humiliation for China in its relations with Japan. At the outbreak of the war, Japan moved against Germany's leased holdings in China's Shandong Province. On 7 November 1914, Japanese gunboats bombarded and seized the port city of Qingdao, where Germany held a concession. The government of warlord Yuan Shikai in Beijing requested that the special transit and military rights held by Germany be returned to China. Japan responded to its notional ally with the Twenty-One Demands, insisting that all German rights in Shandong be turned over to Japan and that Japan enjoy special, and at times, exclusive rights, elsewhere.[9] International pressure whittled the list of demands down to 13, which Beijing accepted on 9 May 1915 with great reluctance.[10] The terms sparked student demonstrations and a boycott of Japanese goods. At the end of the war, the United Kingdom and France excluded China from formal treaty negotiations and confirmed Japan's possessions in Shandong.[11] China's losses were so deeply felt that, from 1927 to 1940, 9 May was commemorated as 'National Humiliation Day'.

The Japanese demands of 1914 and 1915 had profound effects on China's domestic politics. They inspired the populist May Fourth movement of 1919, which ultimately influenced the creation of the Chinese Communist Party (CCP) a decade later. They also provided the context for the founding moment of the People's Republic of China (PRC) in 1949, when Mao Zedong proclaimed: 'Ours will no longer be a nation subject to insult and humiliation. We have stood up.'[12] The phrase 'Never Forget National Humiliation' was first popularised in Chinese newspapers in 1915. It became a slogan 'painted on walls, coined into trademarks and imprinted on stationery', providing a backdrop for future antagonism towards Japan.[13]

Events in the 1930s, particularly the Mukden Incident and the Rape of Nanjing, did much to cement the notion in China of Japan as an expansionist, aggressive power. On 18 September 1931, a small group of army officers from Japan's Kwantung Army blew up a short section of railway near Mukden (modern Shenyang), which was owned and operated by South Manchurian Railway, a Japanese firm operating in China. Using the pretext that Chinese troops were responsible for the explosion, the Kwantung Army moved into Mukden. Within five months, the Japanese army had overrun the entire territory of Manchuria and in March 1932 the puppet state of Manchukuo was created. At the time, Chinese analyses attributed the actions of the Japanese military to a 'militaristic, imperialistic, expansionist' government bent on achieving hegemony over China and the rest of Asia. This line of argument has been replicated in contemporary Chinese debates about Japanese militarism.[14]

Six years after Mukden, the two states were at war. In early July 1937 Japanese forces used a relatively minor clash at the Marco Polo Bridge, west of Beijing, as a pretext for an attack on China and an invasion of its most developed areas. The imperial army moved south from Manchuria to invade China proper and on 13 December captured the Chinese capital Nanjing. Over the next six weeks, Japanese forces massacred military personnel and civilians in large numbers. *New York Times* correspondent F. Tillman Durdin observed at the time: 'The Japanese appear to want the horrors to remain as long as possible, to impress on the Chinese the terrible results of resisting Japan.' The people of Nanking, he added, had become a 'terrorized population who, under alien domination, live in fear of death, torture, and robbery. The graveyard of tens of thousands of Chinese soldiers may also be the graveyard of all Chinese hopes of resisting conquest by Japan.'[15]

The extent of the devastation at Nanjing is the subject of scholarly debate. Historian Glenn Askew's review of the literature notes that China's official figure of 300,000 dead is high compared with other accounts, such as Honda Katsuichi's estimate of a little over 100,000.[16] Such controversies aside, it is a fact that the atrocities in Nanjing in 1937 have been deeply etched into Chinese memories of Japan's history in China. As Askew notes, 'the Nanjing Incident is not only an important episode in Sino-Japanese relations, but is also emerging as a fundamental keystone in the construction of the modern Chinese national identity'.[17] One reason why Nanjing has made such an indelible mark in Chinese consciousness is the fact that Japan had crushed a city touted as the model of a modern China. Nanjing had until 1421 been China's capital under the Ming Dynasty. The city was renowned for its fine architecture and the gracious lifestyle of its merchant classes. As Rana Mitter notes, Nanjing in 1937 had become the symbol of technological and environmental modernity that the Nationalists desired for all of China. Nanjing was never a strategic target for the Japanese; its capture had only symbolic importance. By capturing it, the Japanese would finally 'demonstrate their victory over Chinese nationalism, a force they considered pernicious and alien to their vision of East Asia's future'.[18]

## Path to normalisation (1945–1972)

The period following the end of the Second World War was a time of rapid geopolitical change in Asia. Japan, the wartime aggressor and promoter of the Greater East Asia Co-prosperity Sphere, was subsumed into the American sphere of influence, first under General Douglas MacArthur, the supreme commander for the Allied Powers, and then under the US–Japan alliance. This marked another change in the triangular relationship between China, Japan and the United States. Between

1898 and the 1920s, the US and Japan had worked together to deal with the chaos in China. From the time of Japan's invasion of Manchuria in 1931 to the end of the Second World War in 1945, the US first cooperated with China and then allied with Beijing to resist Japan. In another turnabout, from 1947 to 1972, the US allied itself with Japan to contain both China and the Soviet Union.

Official relations were limited in the immediate post-war years, as China was wracked by civil war while Japan was under Allied occupation until 1952. Neither Tokyo nor Beijing was under any illusions that they could take the Franco-German route to reconciliation, because of the immense suffering that Japan's imperial forces had inflicted upon China during the war. The overall tone and approach to Sino-Japanese relations were set by leaders on both sides. In the 1950s, Japan's policy towards China under the so-called '1955 political system' of the Liberal Democratic Party (LDP) was generally controlled by the 'pragmatist', technocratic mainstream of the party represented by premiers Shigeru Yoshida and Hayato Ikeda.[19] Writing in *Foreign Affairs* in 1951, Yoshida stressed the pragmatism that undergirded Tokyo's relationship with China: 'Red or white, China remains our next-door neighbour. Geography and economic laws will, I believe, prevail in the long run over any ideological differences and artificial trade barriers.'[20] The Yoshida Doctrine held that Japan should follow a low-profile foreign policy and highly constrained defence posture in the context of the US–Japanese alliance, while seeking to build economic and diplomatic ties across East Asia.

Likewise, the Chinese staked out clear-cut general principles towards Japan: they sought to normalise relations between the two countries, restore their friendship and achieve common prosperity. In 1958, Chinese premier Zhou Enlai declared the 'three political principles' he wished Japan to observe in its relations with China: to not regard China as an enemy; to not obstruct normalisation of relations; and to avoid aiding any effort to create 'two Chinas'.[21] When the two countries normalised relations in 1972, Japan accepted all three principles. Tokyo turned out to be a relatively reluctant partner in the Cold War framework for containing China between 1945 and 1972.

The post-war resumption of commercial ties preceded normalisation in the diplomatic sphere. Even before the establishment of the People's Republic of China in 1949, there were negotiations between the CCP and Japan for the restoration of trade. Such trade was started in 1950 and channelled largely through Hong Kong. It was briefly curtailed during the Korean War, when Japan was used as a staging post for US-led forces in the Korean Peninsula, but thereafter and until the normalisation of relations in 1972, Sino-Japanese trade was conducted through three channels – non-official trade agreements, friendship trade and memorandum trade.[22] There were four non-official trade agreements, which involved areas such as barter trade and fishery arrangements. Friendship trade, which involved Chinese designation of 300 Japanese companies as 'friendly firms', was instituted after the United States expressed displeasure over increased non-official trade. Memorandum trade was based on a 1962 bilateral trade agreement known as the 'L-T Memorandum' after its two signatories – Liao Chengzhi, chairman of the China–Japan Friendship Association, and Tatsunosuke Takasaki, a senior LDP parliamentarian.[23]

*The golden triangle (1972–1989)*
Geopolitical changes in the late 1960s made possible the establishment of a 'golden triangle' of relations involving the US, China and Japan, beginning in 1972 and lasting until the 1989 Tiananmen Square protests in Beijing. Washington was seeking

to extract itself from a long, gruelling war in Vietnam and wanted China's help to achieve this and to contain the Soviet Union. China, for its part, was eager to improve ties with the US as a response to a decade-long deterioration in Sino-Soviet relations, which in 1969 had brought the two communist states close to war. These strategic imperatives created the political will for agreements around the Taiwan issue in the early 1970s, in particular Washington's recognition of the 'One China' principle and Beijing's acquiescence to US public reaffirmation of its desire for a peaceful settlement of the Taiwan issue.

Henry Kissinger, Richard Nixon's national security advisor, sought containment as a goal but his chief objective was a 'global equilibrium' – a stable balance of power involving the US, China and the Soviet Union. Kissinger based this on what he called the 'geopolitical tradition'.[24] He calculated that improved Sino-American relations would give Moscow an incentive to improve its relations with the US. Historical experience suggested that, for the US facing two antagonistic powers, it was more advantageous to align with the weaker to restrain the stronger.[25]

Ahead of his meeting with Chinese premier Zhou Enlai in Feburary 1972, President Nixon noted that China was concerned about Japan's growing economic power and committed himself to prevent Japan from building its own nuclear arsenal or stretching out its hands to Korea, Taiwan and Indonesia. In his meeting with the Chinese leader, Nixon sought to convince China that the US–Japanese relationship upheld China's interests, rather than working against them.[26] This theme was to recur in subsequent policy debates. In June 1984, US Assistant Secretary of State for Defense Richard Armitage explained to Congress that Japan's neighbours did not want Japan to play a major military role in the region and so the US would keep Japan on a short leash, despite exhortations that Japan do more strategically.[27] In 1990 the leading US Marine Corps general in Japan stressed that US troops had to remain in the country until the beginning of the twenty-first century, in large part because 'no one wants a rearmed, resurgent Japan. So we are a cap in the bottle, if you will.'[28]

Japanese policymakers felt betrayed by the US–Chinese rapprochement. However, Japan wasted no time in seeking normalisation with China and achieved this on 29 September 1972, more than six years earlier than the US. Normalisation was the logical extension of Japan's policy of quasi-official relations since the 1950s. In common with the US, Japan approached normalisation of relations with China with little regard for the US–Japanese alliance. In the process Tokyo had to employ some diplomatic sleight of hand. For instance, Japan was able to gloss over the problem of Taiwan, a fellow US ally. The prime minister, Kakuei Tanaka, terminated diplomatic ties with Taipei but obtained Beijing's permission to continue economic and other non-political relations.[29] Interestingly, Japan also managed to achieve normalisation with China on its own terms, arguing that the agreement with Beijing did not affect its security alliance with the US; rather, Japan's development of a special relationship with China was independent of strategic considerations.[30]

The establishment of normal relations in 1972 and the conclusion of the Peace and Friendship Treaty in 1978 paved the way for the most successful period in Sino-Japanese relations in the modern era. In December 1979, Japan announced its first Official Development Assistance (ODA) package for China. By 1987, China had overtaken Indonesia to become Japan's leading destination for ODA in terms of annual net yen loan disbursements. Since 1993, China has been the leader in terms of cumulative funds received.[31]

It has been argued that the system of relations established by normalisation privileged sentimentalism over pragmatism and suppressed candid discussion of real bilateral issues with the slogan of friendship.[32] Thus the issue of Japan's atrocities in China in the 1930s and 1940s was shelved, as were territorial disputes. This, however, did not mean that the relationship was devoid of periodic tensions. In 1982, Japan's Education and Culture Ministry softened the treatment of the country's wartime record in some history textbooks. Governments and society in China, South Korea and other Asian countries took offence. In 1985, Japanese Prime Minister Yasuhiro Nakasone visited the Yasukuni Shrine, which honours 2.5 million war dead, including 14 Class A war criminals from the Second World War. The visit sparked widespread demonstrations in China.

*Growing dualism (1990–2010)*

The golden triangle was a product of the Cold War, which by 1989 had largely run its course.[33] In June of that year, student-led demonstrations in Beijing's Tiananmen Square called for government accountability, the eradication of corruption among China's elite and political reform. The authorities responded with a military crackdown that resulted in casualties estimated at several hundred to more than 1,000.[34] At the time, Japan's policy was to draw China further into the global trading system and to downplay the security concerns that occasionally dogged bilateral relations. Following the Tiananmen crackdown, Japan followed America's lead by suspending a $5.5 billion, six-year concessional loan programme to China that had been announced in 1988. Tokyo also withdrew all Japanese experts working on government-funded projects in China and announced a review of Japan's Export–Import Bank policies towards China.[35] Japan sought to limit the damage this would do to bilateral relations. Prime Minister Sosuke Uno refused to characterise Tokyo's steps as sanctions, observing that to impose sanctions would be 'very impolite to a neigh-bouring country'.[36]

Increasingly, cooperative trade and economic relations were accompanied by political tension and competition. Changes in the global power balance proved disruptive too. Whereas in the 1970s the US saw in China a counterweight to the Soviet Union, it now began to view Beijing as a potential competitor; debate raged in Washington over whether to pursue engage-ment, containment or some hybrid in relation to China.[37] The Clinton administration opted principally for engagement, seeking to involve China in as many international regimes as possible. By the late 1990s, however, the US approach also included some hedging against any negative repercussions attached to China's rise. President George W. Bush, who came to office in 2001 calling China a 'strategic competitor', autho-rised the sale of high-tech weapons to Taiwan. Relations were further strained by a collision between a US spy plane and a Chinese fighter jet over the South China Sea in 2001, although thereafter ties were stabilised as the US refocused on the threat of terrorism following the September 11 terrorist attacks on New York and Washington DC. The balanced approach was essentially replicated by Barack Obama. There was some symbiosis in US–China relations, particularly in the financial sphere where China furnished the US with massive capital inflows that enabled US consumers to buy the goods made by Chinese factories. Yet the relationship was becoming one of competitive coexistence. Interests, approaches and policies were diverging rather than converging. As David Shambaugh has noted, there was a fundamental deficit of 'strategic trust'.[38]

Japanese policy followed a similar course to that of the US. By the mid-1990s, Japan had begun to perceive China as less stable, more nationalistic and even eager to confront Japan on various issues. Economically, China was perceived to be failing to conform to Japanese concepts of an orderly production and investment hierarchy in Asia, with Japan heading a 'flock of geese' comprising first the newly industrialised economies, then ASEAN and finally China. China also intruded into what Japan regarded as its own economic space in ASEAN, by concluding bilateral free-trade agreements with Southeast Asian states and promoting an alternative Chinese developmental model based on the 'Beijing consensus'.[39]

Michael Green and Benjamin Self paint a vivid picture of how Japan's foreign policy toward China shifted from 'commercial liberalism' to 'reluctant realism' in the late 1990s, as the four pillars of Japan's policy toward China – security, economics, history and domestic politics – changed. A new set of dynamics in bilateral relations was already discernible. China's continued nuclear testing, its hostility towards Taiwan and the advancement of nationalistic territorial claims cast a 'new light' on its economic growth and apparent inability to move beyond nineteenth-century concepts of state sovereignty.[40] In August 1995, Japan informed China that it would suspend grant assistance to Beijing as a protest against its continued nuclear-weapons testing. In the autumn of that year, Japanese fighter jets scrambled in response to threatening moves by Chinese jets in Japanese airspace. In October 1995, Japanese Foreign Minister Yohei Kono made front-page news in Japan by stating that Chinese military modernisation and territorial policies could be a source of instability in Asia. In early 1996, China became alarmed at what it perceived to be Taiwanese moves towards independence, in the form of preparations for a democratic election and Taiwanese President Lee Teng-Hui's visit to Cornell University in the US. Two weeks before Taiwan's 23 March presidential election, the PLA conducted test-firings of some of its missiles, some of which landed in sea lanes 30 miles off Taiwan's northern port of Keelung and 47 miles from the southern port of Kaohsiung. Maritime shipping and flights were disrupted.[41] This coercive diplomacy showed that Beijing had found the confidence to challenge Taipei, and by extension Washington, bringing China to the brink of conflict with the United States. The implications were not lost on Japanese policymakers. Right-wingers were blunt in their appraisal. Tokyo Governor Shintaro Ishihara described China as the 'biggest military threat in the world'.[42]

At the start of the twenty-first century, Chinese attitudes towards Japan also took on a more competitive and suspicious flavour. China increasingly saw itself as the target of efforts by Tokyo and Washington to strengthen their military alliance. In 1996, President Clinton and Japanese Prime Minister Ryutaro Hashimoto issued a joint declaration on security. Under the revised guidelines for security cooperation, Japan agreed to provide logistical and other non-combat support to US military operations in 'areas surrounding Japan'. This sparked concerns in Beijing over the implications for China's claim to Taiwan.[43] Chinese concerns about the US–Japan alliance worsened as Japan remained ambiguous on the Taiwan issue. It did not give China an explicit promise to exclude Taiwan from the scope of its defence agreement with the United States.[44] In the context of a revived alliance, the presence of US forces seems to China less like a cap in the bottle, to prevent Japan rising, and more like an eggshell, giving Japan protection until it was ready to unleash its military power.[45]

As competitive aspects of the relationship between China and Japan became more prominent, the two countries' contested history and the Senkaku/Diaoyu dispute periodically surfaced. In November 1998, Jiang Zemin became the first Chinese president to visit Japan. The previous month Tokyo had made a written apology to South Korea for its brutal occupation of the peninsula in 1910–45. There was an expectation in China that Tokyo would offer a similar apology to China for Imperial Japan's wartime atrocities, thus putting the thorny issue to rest. Japanese Prime Minister Keizo Obuchi spoke of Japan's remorse and apology, but this was diluted in the written statement, reportedly because China refused to promise that receipt of the apology would mark the end of the matter.[46] Jiang deemed the oral apology insufficient, and proceeded to lecture his hosts about Japan's wartime past. To make things worse, he did so in front of the emperor.[47]

The historiographic dispute gained greater salience during Junichiro Koizumi's term as Japanese prime minister from 2001 to 2006. A charismatic politician who belonged to the revisionist faction of the LDP, Koizumi brought with him neo-liberal prescriptions for Japan's economy and a nationalist agenda. In common with his fellow revisionists, Koizumi was reluctant to submit to China over issues of colonial history, disposed to prefer democratic Taiwan over authoritarian mainland China, and in favour of a larger military role for Japan.[48] Koizumi, who showed a sentimental respect for the sacrifices of the common Japanese soldier, did not shirk from visiting the Yasukuni Shrine despite warnings from advisers that such a visit could damage Japan's relations with China and South Korea. Chinese observers interpreted Koizumi's insistence on visiting Yasukuni as evidence of Tokyo's broader ambitions. One scholar argued that the shrine was a 'political symbol' for an attempt to restore the 'old dream' of Japanese empire. Koizumi, he wrote, aimed to break away from Japan's historical burden of its wartime aggression and realise Japan's aspiration to become a 'political and military power'.[49]

In 2004, seven Chinese activists landed on Uotsuri/Diaoyu Dao, the largest island in the Senkaku/Diaoyu chain, and were arrested by Japanese police. This sparked protests from China's Foreign Ministry, which called it a serious violation of Chinese sovereignty. It was the first time since 1996 that protesters had landed on the islands.

In October 2006, at the beginning of his first term as prime minister, Koizumi's successor Shinzo Abe visited China and the two countries issued a Joint Statement in which they agreed to build a 'mutually beneficial relationship based on common strategic interests'. They sought to diffuse the controversial historical questions by passing them on to a joint committee of historians. Japanese diplomats attached weight to China's formal acknowledgement that Japan had played a part in China's economic reconstruction as well as Tokyo's commitment to peace since 1945. China insisted that its development was peaceful, while Japan announced that it had followed a peaceful path for more than 60 years and would continue to do so. Both countries' sides also agreed that the relationship was important enough that they would operate on 'the two wheels of politics and economics'.

Once the political foundations had been laid, the economics of the relationship were addressed more fully. A raft of commercial agreements followed. They addressed exchanges of communication technology, investment and finance. Joint projects were planned to promote farming, forestry and fishery. In 2008, China and Japan concluded an agreement outlining a framework for exploiting oil and gas resources in the East China Sea. Three factors underpinned the deal: Japan was now under the leadership of a prime minister from the LDP's pro-China faction, Yasuo Fukuda; there were effective diplomatic backchannels between the two countries; and China's president and prime minister, Hu Jintao and Wen Jiabao, sought to promote good relations with Tokyo.[50]

Bilateral relations then took a turn for the worse. The influence of the pro-China faction in the LDP declined, while Hu was replaced by the more hawkish Xi Jinping. The 2010 arrest of a Chinese fishing-trawler captain in the vicinity of the Senkaku/Diaoyu Islands by the Japan Coast Guard (JCG) led to growing acrimony. The 1972 bargain, by which sensitive topics were shelved, had unravelled. Exchanges between the two states were marred by disputes over history, territorial claims, trade and production, developmental paradigms, energy security and military security.[51] According to Christopher Hughes, Japan's policy on China moved from 'reluctant realism' to 'resentful realism', which is characterised by increasing paranoia and unpredictable security behaviour.[52]

## The politics of economic interdependence

Ties between the world's second- and third-largest economies are extensive. China became Japan's biggest trading partner in 2007, overtaking the US, while Japan is China's second-largest trading partner.[53] Bilateral trade in 2010 amounted to $340bn. According to official Chinese data, Japan is the second-largest source of foreign direct investment (FDI) into China, with cumulative flows of $61.2bn. Small and medium companies from Japan have established production chains with Chinese firms. Japan provides the high-technology design and management, with China providing the rest. Economic links have been reinforced by twinning relations between regions and cities in China and Japan. Japanese firms operate more than 22,000 companies in China, employing 10m Chinese workers. Recently, China has begun to invest in Japan as well – reflecting the growing symbiosis in the economic relationship.

After 1945, economic links were rebuilt much faster and further than political relations. From the early 1950s to 1971, the year prior to normalisation of relations, trade was conducted through unofficial channels. A barter trade agreement was signed in 1952, followed by the opening of resident trade missions, which were granted quasi-diplomatic privileges in

1956. Then, and for years afterwards, Japan's government saw bilateral trade as contributing to China's economic development and the prevention of social and political collapse. In 1962, as Sino-Soviet tensions increased, another unofficial trade agreement was concluded: the 'L–T Memorandum', signed by Liao Chengzhi and Tatsunosuke Takasaki.

Bilateral trade took off exponentially following the normalisation of Sino-Japanese relations. Trade turnover increased sixfold between 1972 and 1979, to $6.6bn. While for the US, rapprochement with China was a geopolitical endeavour, for Japan the main objective was to deepen economic relations with China despite the geopolitical constraints. For Japan, China was a vast, untapped market; it also had a resource base that could help alleviate Japanese concerns about security of supply of oil and other raw materials. In a further sign that Japan saw normalisation through the lens of trade and domestic interests rather than foreign and security policy, Tokyo resisted, in protracted negotiations over a peace and friendship treaty, pressure from Beijing to target the Soviet Union.

Beijing, meanwhile, viewed Japan as a model and facilitator for China's own economic modernisation. Chinese leader Deng Xiaoping, who visited Japan in 1978, was impressed by Japan's modernity and advanced technology and wanted China to learn from them. Japan's ODA helped to develop China's infrastructure and modern factories, and provided training in modern industrial skills and management. Most spectacular was the $3.8bn Baoshan steel plant, with an annual capacity of 6m tonnes. As Ezra Vogel observed, 'no country played a greater role in assisting China build its industry and infrastructure than Japan'.[54]

To some extent the two countries did seek to use economic links to achieve political objectives. For China, such links contributed to its economic development and the consolidation of its external environment; for Japan, the interaction helped to prevent a collapse of order in China and gave Chinese policy elites a stake in mitigating nationalistic hostility towards Japan. The growing economic ties failed, however, to prevent politics from affecting the relationship. In 1982, Deng urged that the Chinese people be educated in patriotism. This entailed a shift in emphasis away from socialism, and was triggered by reports of a new Japanese school textbook that whitewashed Japan's past aggression against China. Deng was also angered by Japan's foot-dragging over ODA. He described the aid as something that China was entitled to, given that Beijing had not asked for war reparations when bilateral relations were normalised.

In the wake of the Tiananmen protests in Beijing in June 1989, Japan joined other G7 countries in a statement criticising China, but argued for language on the importance of not isolating China. On 26 June, after a discussion with US President George W. Bush and Secretary of State James Baker in Washington, Japanese Foreign Minister Hiroshi Mitsuzuka said that Japan and the US could not tolerate the Chinese government's abuse of human rights. He added, however, that both countries should not 'push China into a position of isolation'.[55] Two years later Japan resumed aid disbursements to China, and in August 1991 Japanese Prime Minister Toshiki Kaifu became the first G7 leader to visit China after Tiananmen. This was followed by an April 1992 visit to Japan by General Secretary Jiang Zemin. Despite the evident mutual interest in close commercial relations, there were growing political differences. In May 1995, around the time that the Comprehensive Test Ban Treaty was coming into force, Japan realised that it could not use economic levers to persuade China to desist from its nuclear testing. Japan suspended a symbolic

$75m in grant assistance, only to be rebuked by Beijing. China argued that Japan, as a historical aggressor, had no right to protest at what China took to be a defensive move on its part. In 1995 and 1996, China's use of coercive diplomacy to prevent Taiwan from moving towards de facto independence also increased Japanese perceptions of an emerging and assertive China. While trade relations continued apace, neither people-to-people exchanges nor intergovernmental agreements to deepen trade links modified the poor opinions the two populations held of each other.

As the twenty-first century dawned, economic interdependence grew but continued to do little to improve diplomatic and political relations. The 2010 arrest of the Chinese fishing-vessel captain who had collided with two JCG ships near the Senkaku/Diaoyu Islands angered Beijing. A Chinese minister issued a vague warning about economic consequences, and China exploited its near-monopoly on rare-earth mineral production to punish Japan. Tokyo's nationalisation of the islands in September 2012 led to protests which closed down some Japanese factories in China.

As Michael Yahuda summarises the limited impact of dense commercial ties on Sino-Japanese relations:

> it could seem that the deepening economic interdependence between China and Japan has not brought about a resolution of the deep political and security divisions between the two. Nor would it seem to have increased mutual trust and understanding between the two peoples. Yet the bureaucratic and business elites of both countries have successfully intensified their mutually dependent economic relations to the extent that neither side has allowed mutual antipathies to stand in the way of economic exchanges.[56]

Some academics argue that economic interdependence is a source of peace.[57] Richard Katz argues that a measure of restraint in the behaviour of Japan and China since the start of Abe's second stint as prime minister is attributable to economic interests or, as he puts it, 'mutual assured production'.[58] However, the thesis that trade promotes peace is problematic. Britain and Germany enjoyed a deep trading relationship in the years prior to the outbreak of the First World War.[59] Dale C. Copeland suggests that trade expectations might matter more for the maintenance of peace: when expectations for trade expansion are positive, leaders have less reason to seek war. If they are pessimistic about trade prospects, then economic calculations are less likely to exert a restraining influence.[60] If this is correct, the downturn in trade and investment between China and Japan in 2012–13 may be a cause for concern. Bilateral trade fell 5.1% year on year in 2013, having contracted by 3.9% in 2012. Japanese direct investment in China fell 4.3% in 2013, even as total FDI in China rose, while direct Chinese investment in Japan fell 23.5% (again, in the context of an overall increase in outbound investment). In addition, long-term trends in China will see 'delinkage' between the two economies. China's increasingly strict enforcement of labour and environmental laws could dampen Japanese investment further.[61] Borrowing from Copeland's theory of trade expectations, Gordon Chang argues that nations will have less interest in each other's success when their economies are pulling apart.[62]

Even if the costs of war are considerable, the risk of conflict cannot be ruled out altogether, particularly in a region where the concept of national honour looms large.[63] Honour and fear colour perceptions of what may look like objective interests.[64] Third-wave critiques of classical deterrence theory argue that countries can rationally go to war based on different values and goals from their deterrers, and hence deterrence can fail.

Such parties are rational – at least in a limited sense – but they behave strategically in ways that are unreasonable.[65]

The Arab attack on Israel in October 1973 surprised Tel Aviv and Washington because the Arabs were waging a war to 'restore self-respect' – a value not understood or shared by the Israelis and Americans. The same might apply to the current Sino-Japanese context. From a Western perspective, a Chinese move to seize the Senkaku/Diaoyu Islands might be irrational, as it would trigger a military response from the US–Japanese alliance. Yet Chinese decision-makers might see the choice differently, based on the need to reclaim China's position and prestige after a 'Century of Humiliation'.

## The burdens of history

The period between 1895 and 1945, when Japan encroached deep into China, left indelible wounds on the Chinese national psyche. Both powers suffered defeat and humiliation at the hands of Western powers in the mid-nineteenth century. Japan was coerced into opening itself to global trade by the US, while China's Qing Dynasty was defeated by the British in the First Opium War. Their responses in the face of Western encroachment differed sharply. China resisted opening up to Western ways, influences and technology. Japan adopted a different coping strategy, embracing Western political and economic concepts vigorously. It followed nineteenth-century educator and diplomat Yukichi Fukuzawa's dictum, 'Leave Asia, enter the West'.[66] The Meiji Restoration put Japan on a much higher growth and modernisation trajectory than China, and it enabled Japan to inflict on China the humiliation it had itself experienced in 1853. These humiliations included the 1895 Treaty of Shimonoseki; the transfer to Japan of Germany's rights in Shandong during the First World War; the Mukden Incident and the Nanjing Massacre;

and the subsequent occupation of much of China by Japanese imperial forces.

Japan's proximity to China, the cultural similarities that the Japanese share with the Chinese, and Japan's extensive interactions with China in the modern period justify its designation as 'China's Occident'. Chinese nationalists use Japan and 'the Occident' to build their own visions of China and its proper place in the world.[67] China, meanwhile, has served as 'Japan's Orient' and has helped the Japanese to construct their own sense of a modern, oriental Japanese nation.[68] It is thus easy to understand the sense of betrayal that the Chinese felt when considering the atrocities that Japan inflicted upon China. In Chinese eyes, Japan was a similar but inferior culture.[69] The similarity and closeness of Japan made the defeats for China much more difficult to bear than losses to 'Western barbarians'. Many Chinese today see the 1895 loss to Japan and the resulting Treaty of Shimonoseki as the darkest hour in the 'Century of Humiliation'.[70] In his 1997 diatribe *Why Japan Won't Settle Accounts*, Li Zhengtang argues that for hundreds of years China was Japan's 'benevolent teacher'. In the Sino-Japanese War of 1895, however, 'China lost to her "student"'. He then asks, 'How can we sons and grandsons of the Yellow Emperors forget for a moment this great racial insult?'[71]

The traumas of the 1930s forged part of modern Chinese identity. Zheng Wang argues that group identity is created in large part by certain struggles that a group has endured. These struggles can be classified as 'chosen traumas' and 'chosen glories'.[72] China's 'chosenness' stems from the belief that China is the centre of the universe; it was believed that whoever controlled Zhongguo, or the Central Kingdom, would be the legitimate ruler of *tianxia*, or the 'realm under heaven'. Chinese myths such as 'civilised ancient nation' (*wenming guguo*) and 'nation of ritual and etiquette' (*liyizhibang*) lie at the centre of

China's identity education. Lastly, the discourse of the 'Century of Humiliation' – China's defeat and shame at the hands of foreign powers from 1845 to 1945 – is used as the master narrative of Chinese history.[73]

## Saving face

The idea of China's perceived superiority over Japan can also be examined via the concept of 'face', or pride, dignity or prestige.[74] Peter Hays Gries notes that Chinese views of face can be understood on two levels: *lian* (decency or good moral reputation) and *mianzi* (extra reputation achieved through social accomplishments). Focusing on the latter, he argues that face between two countries is a battle over the 'zero sum resource of social status'. Thus face is 'fundamentally political, involving a contest over power. Parties vie for face.'[75]

Contemporary Chinese people view global diplomacy as a fierce competition for status and hierarchical position. Hu Jintao's 1996 visit to the US was poorly received back in China, because it was not an official 'state visit' and the Chinese president was subject to minor indignities while there.[76] The importance China attaches to face magnified the significance of these shortcomings. By contrast, Hu's 2011 visit was well received in China as it had the status of a full state visit, with a 21-gun salute and a state dinner.[77]

There is also an element of morality attached to Chinese conceptions of face, as Wang has noted. In May 1999, NATO jets mistakenly bombed the Chinese Embassy in Belgrade, leading to three Chinese deaths. Then in April 2001, a US EP-3E *Aries* II aircraft on a routine surveillance mission collided with a Chinese J-8 fighter, whose pilot died. In both cases, China managed to extract apologies from Washington that it manipulated for consumption by its own public. President George W. Bush had said he was 'very sorry' for the EP-3 incident, but

Beijing translated 'very sorry' into *'shenbiao qianyi'* – an expression of deep apology or regret that Washington had deliberately avoided.[78] Lucian Pye explains the Chinese thinking:

> When the Chinese have the moral high ground, they can be unrelenting in exploiting the situation. It goes back to the Confucian tradition, in which the ruler is morally superior, and therefore when your opponent apologizes it proves they are morally inferior and cannot be the legitimate ruler.[79]

Chinese concerns, even obsession, over conceptions of superiority and face lead to an inclination to link current events – particularly events that relate to Japan – to historical analogies.[80] In 1990, for example, Deng drew a parallel between the West's imposition of sanctions in the wake of the Tiananmen Square massacre to the invasion of China by eight allied Western powers in 1900.[81] In 2002, Zhao Wei, a famous Chinese actress, donned a dress emblazoned with the design of the wartime Japanese Imperial flag, leading to widespread protests in China's blogosphere and media. The *Chengdu Daily* drew an analogy with the 1937 Nanjing massacre, printing 'An Open Letter from Nanjing Massacre Survivors to Zhao Wei'.[82]

According to William Callahan, China's humiliation discourse involves a very active concept of history and recovery. The narrative behind Mao's 1949 statement that China had 'stood up' is one of national salvation, which had been preceded by national humiliation.[83] For decades, the CCP's legitimacy rested on two pillars: Marxism–Leninism and nationalism. China's selective embrace of economic reform and globalisation has greatly devalued the first pillar, leaving nationalism to bear a greater weight. The politicisation of history within the education syllabus and public life has become a key aspect of

Chinese nationalism.[84] As others in Asia have noted, China's patriotic education syllabus was launched in 1994 in an attempt to educate young Chinese on the atrocities committed by the Japanese.[85]

Since Abe's return for his second term as Japanese prime minister in December 2012, his penchant for underscoring Japan's pride of place in the global community has accentuated Chinese fears about a Japanese reversion to militarism. Since taking office, Abe has pursued a reinterpretation of Japan's pacifist constitution to allow for a more robust role in collective-defence arrangements.[86] To many Chinese observers, Abe's actions are incontrovertible evidence that he is on a right-wing, militarist path. In May 2013, Abe appeared in the cockpit of a fighter jet bearing the number 731. In an unfortunate coincidence, it was the Japanese Imperial Army's Unit 731 that had conducted heinous medical experiments in China during the Second World War. South Korea's largest-circulation newspaper *Chosun Ilbo* said Abe's 'numerical provocations' made him the most reviled politician in the country.[87] In August 2013, the Japan Maritime Self Defense Force (JMSDF) launched the 27,000-tonne helicopter carrier *Izumo* – the biggest warship unveiled in Japan since the Second World War. The carrier's chosen name was unfortunate; a carrier of the same name attacked China during the war.[88]

By far the most provocative comments, to Chinese ears, were those made by Taro Aso, a former Japanese prime minister and finance minister. Speaking to a gathering of LDP supporters in July 2013, Aso appeared to praise the National Socialists' undermining of Germany's interwar constitution. Their methods, he suggested, could serve as a model for Japanese conservatives as they sought to revise the country's Basic Law.[89] Aso later backtracked from his remarks but this did little to limit the fallout.[90] In August 2013, many media outlets in Asia were quick to point out that Abe omitted any expressions of remorse for Japan's wartime military aggression in Asia on the anniversary of Japan's surrender on 15 August 1945. A tradition of expressing remorse has been followed by every prime minister since Tomiichi Murayama's historic 1995 'Murayama Statement'. Moreover, it was noted that Abe did not repeat the pledge that Japan would never go to war again – a pledge he had made in 2007 during his first term.[91]

Chinese observers interpret the actions and comments made by Abe and his cabinet as evidence that Japan has reverted to a path of militarism. Some have even questioned Abe's mental health.[92] There is also a suspicion among Chinese analysts that Abe is exaggerating the Chinese threat in order to gain more attention from and influence over the US as it rebalances to Asia. They note that, while other Asian states favour a deeper strategic dialogue between the US and China, Japan sees the rebalance in antagonistic terms, as an opportunity to pursue its own security agenda and intensify tensions between Beijing and Washington.[93] Such analysts construe even relatively concilia-tory moves by Japan negatively. At the Shangri-La Dialogue in Singapore in June 2013, for example, Japanese Defense Minister Itsunori Onodera spoke about a 'strong Japan' making a 'peace-ful contribution' to regional and global security. Addressing the widespread view that the Abe administration had made a swing to the revisionist right, Onodera said that such views were 'total misperceptions'. He then invoked the spirit of Murayama's 1995 statement, telling the 350 delegates at the Dialogue that Japan had 'caused tremendous damage and suffering to the people of many countries'.[94] Chinese analysts in Beijing felt that Onodera was merely 'mouthing the words' of the 1995 Murayama Statement without really meaning them. Some even argue that Japan has *never* apologised for its wartime atrocities, given that the word *daoqian* ('apology') used in Murayama's statement was the mild form, rather than the stronger *xiezui* ('apologise for an offence').

This underlines the difficulty of achieving reconciliation given the prevalence of nationalist feeling in both countries. China continues to insist that Japan 'come clean' about its wartime atrocities, not least because China's nationalist discourse focuses on the need to correct past wrongs during the 'Century of Humiliation'.[95] If Japan does not apologise for its wartime transgressions, it stands accused of refusing to accept its historical debt. If it does apologise, it risks being accused of insincerity. As Yinan He notes:

> Whenever there is a conflict of interest with Japan, the Chinese people always expect Japan to make concessions because it owed China so much throughout history. If the Japanese side does not yield, this will feed into the Chinese perception of hostile Japanese intentions: in instances of economic friction, the Chinese people suspect that the reason that Japan refuses to make concessions is because it is trying to make a profit at the expense of Chinese economic interests; in a sovereignty dispute, they suspect that Japan has territorial or other strategic ambitions against China. If the Chinese government wants to compromise, then public rage will quickly turn against the 'traitorous' government. In order to placate public anger and deflect anti-establishment challenges, the government has to maintain a hard-line policy towards Japan. This is why Chinese popular nationalism can significantly increase bilateral tension at the official level. [96]

Meanwhile, Japan wishes to shake off the sins of the past and to re-emerge as a confident, active economic and political actor following two decades of economic stagnation. Tokyo displays growing signs of apology fatigue, manifested in an indifference to, and even resentment of, foreigners' hectoring on historical issues.[97] Japanese officials would say that Japan is a 'country with a long history and a short memory'.[98] Japanese analysts admit that careless comments made by Abe and his cabinet colleagues have been unhelpful, and they dismiss Aso's suggestion that Japan should emulate Nazi Germany on the constitutional question. However, Japan will not follow the German model of expiation and no Japanese premier is likely to make an apology for the country's wartime record that would match the one offered by German Chancellor Willy Brandt. To do so would be to condemn the memory of the Japanese soldiers who died during the war, and more importantly, challenge the imperial system that the Americans as occupiers allowed to continue after the surrender of Japan in August 1945. Thus a proper recognition of Japan's militarist past would put into question the modern Japan – a constitutional monarchy with the emperor as head of state.[99] John Dower argues that negative impressions of Japan as an aggressor in the wars of the mid-twentieth century run so deep that post-war Japanese have been unable to look upon their modern history and accomplishments with pride.[100] The Japanese are frustrated by the refusal of China to acknowledge Japan's contrition over its wartime record, as well as China's disinclination to credit Japan for its peaceful post-war development and its contribution to China's economic development since 1972.[101]

When he visited the Yasukuni Shrine in 1985, Nakasone said that the Tokyo War Crimes Trials had 'spread throughout Japan a self-torturing belief that our country was to blame for everything'. He challenged this, saying that Japan had to 'cast disgrace aside, (advance) forward in the pursuit of glory – this is the essence of the nation and of the people'.[102] Abe has adopted a similar tack in his narrative about Japanese revival. On the Japanese side, a denial of history facilitates Abe's grand goals of restoring Japanese pride and setting Japan on the path of normalisation. In a February 2013 speech in Washington, he made an explicit link between economic resuscitation and a strong defence. Japan is not and will never be a tier-two country, he stressed.[103]

Chinese analysts are fairly realistic about Japanese apologies. To them, the Japanese might have a natural reluctance to apologise further, given that an honest admission to all the atrocities committed by Japanese forces during the Second World War could effect 'tremendous trauma' on the Japanese people. According to one Chinese source, this is evident in the trauma experienced by Japanese youths when they visit the Anti-Japanese Museum in Beijing – a museum that depicts in stark and graphic detail the atrocities committed by the Japanese. That said, Chinese analysts said that it would be better for the Japanese people to suffer some short-term pain before the pain goes away eventually.[104] If the heads of Japanese companies can apologise for various infractions, Japanese politicians can do likewise.

It should be noted that, although Abe took office for the second time in December 2012, he did not immediately act on the revisionist promises made during his campaign. He waited a year before visiting the Yasukuni Shrine and did not, as of September 2014, revise the 1995 Murayama Statement.

Nevertheless, his refusal or inability to rein in ministers who make revisionist comments about history, and to stop Japanese politicians visiting Yasukuni Shrine, are a continued bugbear in Sino-Japanese relations. In March 2014, Abe sought to press on with his bid to reinterpret Article 9 of the constitution, despite opposition from his own LDP. If successful, Japan would for the first time be able to formally exercise collective defence – that is, come to the assistance of the United States in the event of an attack on the latter.[105] Chinese observers argue that the residual goodwill that had resulted from the 1995 Murayama Statement has been undermined by what they perceive to be a lack of sincerity and contrition on Japan's part.

## Notes

1   Katherine Burns, 'China and Japan: Economic Relationship to Political Ends', in Michael Krepon and Chris Gagné (eds), *Economic Confidence-Building and Regional Security*, report no. 36 (Washington DC: Stimson Center, October 2000), p. 28.

2   Unless otherwise stated, this section on Sino-Japanese relations before 1895 is based on *ibid.*; Caroline Rose, *Interpreting History in Sino-Japanese Relations: A Case Study in Political Decision-Making* (London: Routledge, 1998), pp. 4–21; and Eric Teo-Chu Cheow, *Sino-Japanese Relations: Conflict Management and Resolution*, Silk Road Paper (Washington DC and Uppsala: Central Asia-Caucasus Institute and Silk Road Studies Program, December 2006).

3   Nassrine Azimi, 'Ancient Neighbours, Current Antagonists', *New York Times*, 5 November 2010; Tommy Koh, 'China and Japan: Frenemies?', *Straits Times*, 10 April 2013.

4   *Ibid.*

5   Cheow, *Sino-Japanese Relations*, p. 14.

6   John K. Fairbank and Kwang-Ching Liu, *The Cambridge History of China, Vol. 11: Late Ch'ing, 1800–1991, Part 2* (Cambridge: Cambridge University Press, 1980), p. 269.

7   *Ibid.*

8   John Dower, *Embracing Defeat: Japan in the Wake of World War II* (New York: W.W. Norton & Company, 1999), p. 96.

9   Allen S. Whiting, *China Eyes Japan* (Berkeley, CA: University of California Press, 1989), p. 33.

10  Zheng Wang, *Never Forget National Humiliation: Historical Memory in Chinese Politics and Foreign Relations* (New York: Columbia University Press, 2012), loc. 1378 (Kindle edition).

11  Robert H. Wade, 'China–Japan Island Dispute: The Other Side of the Story', *Economic and Political Weekly*, vol. 47, no. 10, 9 March 2013, pp. 27–31.

12  William Callahan, 'National Insecurities: Humiliation, Salvation and Chinese Nationalism', *Alternatives*, vol. 29, no. 2, March–May 2004, p. 203.

13  *Ibid.*, p. 210.

14  Whiting, *China Eyes Japan*, pp. 35–6.

15  F. Tillman Durdin, 'All Captives Slain', *New York Times*, 18 December 1937.

16  Katsuichi told Frank Gibney, who penned the introduction to his work, that the actual figure would not approach 200,000. See Honda Katsuichi, *The Nanjing Massacre: A Japanese Journalist Confronts Japan's National Shame* (Armonk, NY: M.E. Sharpe, 1998), p. xiii.

17 Glenn Askew, 'The Nanjing Incident: Recent Research and Trends', *Electronic Journal of Contemporary Japanese Studies*, vol. 2, no. 1, 4 April 2002, http://www.japanesestudies.org.uk/articles/Askew.html.

18 Rana Mitter, *Forgotten Ally: China's World War II, 1937–1945* (Boston: Houghton Mifflin Harcourt, 2013), loc. 2406–7 (Kindle edition).

19 Christopher Hughes, 'Japan's Response to China's Rise: Regional Engagement, Global Containment, Dangers of Collision', *International Affairs*, vol. 85, no. 4, July 2009, p. 839. For a chronological list of the leaders of China and Japan in the post-war period, see Tables 1 and 2.

20 Shigeru Yoshida, 'Japan and the Crisis in Asia', *Foreign Affairs*, vol. 29, no. 2, January 1951, p. 179.

21 Quansheng Zhao, *Japanese Policymaking: The Politics behind Politics: Informal Mechanisms and the Making of China Policy* (Oxford: Oxford University Press, 1993), pp. 25–7.

22 *Ibid.*, p. 26.

23 *Ibid*, pp. 26–7.

24 Henry Kissinger, *White House Years* (Boston, MA: Little Brown, 1979), pp. 55, 914.

25 *Ibid.*, pp. 177–9, 191–2.

26 James Mann, *About Face: A History of America's Curious Relationship with China, from Nixon to Clinton* (New York: Alfred Knopf, 1998), pp. 43–4.

27 Richard Samuels, *Securing Japan: Tokyo's Grand Strategy and the Future of East Asia* (Ithaca, NY and London: Cornell University Press, 2007), p. 44.

28 Kenneth Pyle, *Japan Rising: The Resurgence of Japanese Power and Purpose* (New York: Public Affairs, 2007), loc. 7284 (Kindle edition).

29 Burns, 'China and Japan: Economic Relationship to Political Ends', p. 40.

30 Soeya Yoshihide, 'Japan's Relations with China', in Ezra Vogel, Yuan Ming and Tanaka Akihiko (eds), *The Golden Age of the U.S.–China–Japan Triangle, 1972–1989* (Cambridge, MA: Harvard University Asia Center, 2002), p. 213.

31 Burns, 'China and Japan: Economic Relationship to Political Ends', p. 45.

32 Ming Wan, *Sino-Japanese Relations: Interaction, Logic, and Transformation* (Washington DC: Woodrow Wilson Center Press, 2006), p. 84.

33 Ezra F. Vogel, 'Introduction', in Vogel, Ming and Akihiko (eds), *The Golden Age of the U.S–China–Japan Triangle*, p. 8.

34 Nicholas Kristof, 'A Reassessment of How Many Died in the Military Crackdown in Beijing', *New York Times*, 21 June 1989.

35 Emma Chanlett-Avery, Kerry Dumbaugh and William H. Cooper, *Sino-Japanese Relations: Issues for U.S. Policy*, CRS Report for Congress R40093 (Washington DC: Congressional Research Service, 19 December 2008), p. 7.

36 *Ibid.*

37 The literature on the containment/engagement debate in the 1990s is vast. See, for example, Christopher Layne, 'From Preponderance to Offshore Balancing. America's Future Grand Strategy', *International Security*, vol. 22, no.1, Summer 1997, pp. 86–124; Gerald Segal, 'East Asia and the "Constrainment" Of China', *International Security*, vol. 20, no. 4, Winter 1995, pp. 107–35; David

Shambaugh, 'Containment or Engagement of China? Calculating Beijing's Responses', *International Security*, vol. 21, no. 2, Fall 1996, pp. 180–209.

[38] David Shambaugh (ed.), *Tangled Titans: The United States and China* (New York: Rowman & Littlefield, 2012), loc. 624–6 (Kindle edition).

[39] Hughes, 'Japan's Response to China's Rise', p. 841.

[40] Michael J. Green and Benjamin L. Self, 'Japan's Changing China Policy: From Commercial Liberalism to Reluctant Realism', *Survival*, vol. 38, no. 2, Summer 1996, pp. 35–58.

[41] Andrew Scobell, 'Show of Force: Chinese Soldiers, Statesmen and the 1995–1996 Taiwan Strait Crisis', *Political Science Quarterly*, vol. 115, no. 2, Summer 2000, pp. 236–8; Andrew Scobell, *China's Military Use of Force: Beyond the Great Wall and the Long March* (Cambridge, MA: Cambridge University Press, 2003), pp. 181–4.

[42] 'Governor of Tokyo Warns of Threat from China', *Financial Times*, 27 April 2000.

[43] Ministry of Foreign Affairs of Japan, 'The Guidelines for Japan–U.S. Defense Cooperation', http://www.mofa.go.jp/region/n-america/us/security/guideline2.html.

[44] 'Why China Wants to Cuddle', *The Economist*, 15 November 1997, pp. 39–40.

[45] Thomas J. Christensen, 'China, the U.S.–Japan Alliance and the Security Dilemma in East Asia', *International Security*, vol. 23, no. 4, Spring 1999, p. 62.

[46] Gao Dexiang, 'Memory, Reconciliation and Chosen Traumas: The Political Psychology of the Chinese State, Media and Public on Sino-Japanese Relations', thesis submitted for degree of Master of Social Sciences, Department of Political Science, National University of Singapore, 2008, p. 70.

[47] *Ibid.*, p. 68; 'Japan, China Keen to Avoid 1998 Jiang Visit Rerun', *Reuters*, 4 May 2008.

[48] Hughes, 'Japan's Response to China's Rise', p. 841.

[49] He Xiaosong, 'Why Koizumi Runs Counter to Public Will?', *People's Daily*, 28 July 2006, http://english.people.com.cn/200607/28/eng20060728_287639.html.

[50] Interviews in Beijing and Tokyo, August–September 2013.

[51] Hughes, 'Japan's Response to China's Rise', p. 842.

[52] Christopher Hughes, 'Japan's Foreign Policy for a New Age: Realistic Realism', *Asahi Shimbun*, 26 February 2011. See also William Choong, 'Stoking Old Flames in New Japan', *Straits Times*, 7 January 2013.

[53] Unless otherwise stated, this section draws on Michael Yahuda, *Sino-Japanese Relations After the Cold War: Two Tigers Sharing a Mountain* (Abingdon: Routledge, 2013), pp. 64–79; Whiting, *China Eyes Japan*, pp. 93–106; Chanlett-Avery, Dumbaugh and Cooper, *Sino-Japanese Relations: Issues for U.S. Policy* pp. 11–17; Burns, 'China and Japan: Economic Relationship to Political Ends', pp. 27–58; and Zhao, *Japanese Policymaking*, pp. 23–9.

[54] Ezra Vogel, *Deng Xiaoping and the Transformation of China* (Cambridge, MA: Harvard University Press,

2011), p. 310, cited in Yahuda, *Sino-Japanese Relations After the Cold War*, p. 70.

55  Tsukasa Takamine, *Japan's Development Aid to China: The Long-Running Foreign Policy of Engagement* (Abingdon: Routledge, 2006), pp. 57–8.

56  Yahuda, *Sino-Japanese Relations After the Cold War*, p. 79.

57  Amy King, 'Japan and China: Warm Trade Ties Temper Political Tensions', *East Asia Forum Quarterly*, vol. 4, no. 3, July–September 2012.

58  Richard Katz, 'Mutual Assured Production: Why Trade Will Limit Conflict Between China and Japan', *Foreign Affairs*, vol. 92, no. 4, July–August 2013, pp. 18–24.

59  David M. Rowe, 'The Trade and Security Paradox in International Politics', unpublished manuscript, Ohio State University, 15 September 1994, p. 16, cited in Samuel Huntington, *The Clash of Civilisations and the Remaking of the World Order* (New York: Simon & Schuster, 1996), p. 67.

60  Dale C. Copeland, 'Economic Interdependence and War: A Theory of Trade Expectations', *International Security*, vol. 20, no. 4, Spring 1996, pp. 5–41.

61  Gordon Chang, 'The Chinese and Japanese Economies are Delinking: Prelude to Conflict?', *Forbes*, 16 February 2014.

62  *Ibid.*

63  James. R. Holmes, 'Economic Interdependence = Less Conflict?' *The Diplomat*, 11 April 2013.

64  *Ibid.*

65  Colin Gray, *Maintaining Effective Deterrence* (Carlisle, PA: Strategic Studies Institute, August 2003);

Colin Gray, 'The Reformation of Deterrence: Moving On', *Comparative Strategy*, vol. 22, no. 5, December 2003, p. 443; Keith B. Payne, *The Fallacies of Cold War Deterrence and a New Direction* (Lexington, KY: University Press of Kentucky, 2001), p. 7; Keith B. Payne, 'The Fallacies of Cold War Deterrence and a New Direction', *Comparative Strategy*, vol. 22, no. 5, December 2003, pp. 411–28.

66  Green and Self, 'Japan's Changing China Policy', p. 40.

67  Peter Hays Gries, *China's New Nationalism: Pride, Politics, and Diplomacy* (Berkeley, CA: University of California Press, 2004), loc. 418–23 (Kindle edition).

68  *Ibid.*

69  Jonathan D. Spence, *The Search for Modern China* (New York: W.W. Norton & Company, 1990), p. 122, cited in Mitter, *Forgotten Ally*, loc. 368 (Kindle edition).

70  Gries, *China's New Nationalism,* loc. 843 (Kindle edition).

71  *Ibid.*, loc. 471 (Kindle edition).

72  Wang, *Never Forget National Humiliation*, loc. 531 (Kindle edition).

73  *Ibid.*, locs 293–1471 (Kindle edition).

74  China Mike, 'The Cult of "Face"', China-mike.com, http://www.china-mike.com/chinese-culture/understanding-chinese-mind/cult-of-face/.

75  Gries, *China's New Nationalism*, loc. 315 (Kindle edition).

76  Joseph Kahn, 'In Hu's Visit to the U.S., Small Gaffes May Overshadow Small Gains', *New York Times*, 22 April 2006.

77  China Mike, 'The Cult of "Face"'.

78  Wang, *Never Forget National Humiliation,* loc. 3723 (Kindle edition).

79 Fox Butterfield, 'China's Demand for Apology Is Rooted in Tradition', *New York Times*, 7 April 2001.

80 Khong uses the concept of analogies to describe how policymakers use lessons in their foreign-policy decision-making. For example, in 1950, the Truman administration reversed its previous assessment that the Korean Peninsula was unimportant to US security because it saw North Korea's invasion of the South as analogous to the actions of Mussolini. See Yuen Foong Khong, *Analogies at War: Korea, Munich, Dien Bien Phu and the Vietnam Decisions of 1965* (Princeton, NJ: Princeton University Press, 1992), pp. 1–9.

81 Deng Xiaoping, 'We Are Working to Revitalise the Chinese Nation', Excerpt from a Talk with Leading Members of the Central Committee, 7 April 1990, *Selected Works of Deng Xiaoping. Vol. 3.* http://archive.org/stream/SelectedWorksOfDeng XiaopingVol.3/Deng03_djvu.txt.

82 'Nanjing datusha xingcunzhe lianming xiegei Zhao Wei de yifeng gongkaixin' (An Open Letter from Nanjing Massacre survivors to Zhao Wei), reprinted at http://www.people.com.cn/BIG5/guandian/183/7087/7090/20011206/620666.html.

83 Callahan, 'National Insecurities', p. 203.

84 Shunji Cui, 'Problems of Nationalism and Historical Memory in China's Relations with Japan', *Journal of Historical Sociology*, vol. 25, no. 2, June 2012, p. 207; Yinan He, 'History, Chinese Nationalism and the Emerging Sino-Japanese Conflict', *Journal of Contemporary China*, vol. 16, no. 50, February 2007, p. 6.

85 'Anti-Japan Mood Seen Keeping Japan, China Apart', *Kyodo News*, 15 September 2004, available at http://www.thefreelibrary.com/TokyoNow%253A+Anti-Japan+mood+seen+keeping+Japan,+China+apart.-a0122269102; Peh Shing Huei, 'Give Credit Where It's Due', *Straits Times*, 28 March 2011.

86 'Redemption', *The Economist*, 27 July 2013; Gerald L. Curtis, 'Japan's Cautious Hawks: Why Tokyo is Unlikely to Pursue an Aggressive Foreign Policy', *Foreign Affairs*, vol. 92, no. 2, March–April 2013, pp. 77–86.

87 Alastair Gale, 'South Korea Media Blast Abe's Numerical Provocations', Wall Street Journal Blog, 15 May 2013, http://blogs.wsj.com/korearealtime/2013/05/15/south-korean-media-blast-abes-numerical-provocations/.

88 'New Japanese Helicopter Carrier Draws China Warning to Asia', Bloomberg.com, 7 August, 2013; 'Intentions Harbored by Japan in its Launch of "Izumo" Warship', *China Military Online*, 7 August 2013.

89 Jonathan Soble, 'Nazi Gaffe Exposes Constitutional Ambition of Japan's LDP', *Financial Times*, 1 August 2013.

90 Isabel Reynolds, 'Abe Hedges Visit to War-Dead Shrine Amid Regional Tension', Bloomberg.com, 14 August 2013.

91 'Abe Ditches Tradition of Expressing Remorse for WWII', *Chosun Ilbo*, 16 August 2013; 'By Omitting Words, Abe Speaks Volumes', *Japan Times*, 15 August 2013; 'Abe Omits Phrases of Remorse for WWII Acts', *Straits Times*, 16 August 2013; 'No Remorse as Abe Marks Surrender', *Xinhua*, 16 August 2013.

92 Author's interviews in Beijing, August 2013.

93 *Ibid.*

94 William Choong, 'Lessons from the Past', Global Politics and Strategy Blog, 1 June 2013, http://www.iiss.org/en/politics%20and%20strategy/blogsections/2013-98d0/may-2aed/japan-aa06.

95 Takashi Inoguchi, 'Four Japanese Scenarios for the Future', *International Affairs*, vol. 65, no. 1, Winter 1988–89, pp. 15–28.

96 He, "History, Chinese Nationalism and the Emerging Sino-Japanese Conflict', pp. 9–10.

97 Daniel Nagashima, 'Japan's Militarist Past: Reconciliation in East Asia?', *Yale Journal of International Affairs*, Fall–Winter 2006, p. 117; John Miller, 'Japan's Burden of History – Can It Be Lifted?', Asia-Pacific Center for Security Studies Occasional Paper, October 2002, p. 8.

98 Thomas Christensen, 'China, the U.S.–Japan Alliance and the Security Dilemma in East Asia', p. 53; Whiting, *China Eyes Japan*, p. 41.

99 Interviews in Tokyo, September 2013. See also Nagashima, 'Japan's Militarist Past', p. 116.

100 John Dower, *Ways of Forgetting, Ways of Remembering: Japan in the Modern World* (New York: New Press, 2012), loc. 1702 (Kindle edition).

101 Richard C. Bush, *The Perils of Proximity: China–Japan Security Relations* (Washington DC: Brookings Institution Press, 2010), loc. 408 (Kindle edition).

102 Yinan He, 'National Mythmaking and the Problems of History in Sino-Japanese Relations', paper presented at the Conference on Memory of War, MIT, 24–25 January 2003, http://web.mit.edu/rpeters/papers/yinan_sino-japanese.pdf.

103 Jonathan Soble, 'Abe Lays Out Vision of Japan Power in Asia', *Financial Times*, 22 February 2013; David Pilling, 'China and the Post-Tsunami Spirit Have Revived Japan', *Financial Times*, 8 May 2013.

104 Interviews in Beijing, August 2013.

105 Kwan Weng Kin, 'Abe Comes Under Opposition in Bid to Reinterpret Constitution', *Straits Times*, 19 March 2014.

# CHAPTER TWO

# The Senkaku/Diaoyu dispute

The Senkaku/Diaoyu Islands comprise five islets and three rocks in the East China Sea about 200km northeast of Taiwan, 400km west of Okinawa and 300km east of the Chinese mainland (see Map 2).[1] They lie at the southern end and on the Chinese side of the Okinawa Trough, a basin that forms the deepest part of the East China Sea. The largest of them, Uotsuri/Diaoyu Dao, has an area of just 4.3km$^2$ and is 383m above sea level at its highest point. The islands lie at the southwestern tip of what the Japanese call the Nansei-shoto or Nansei Islands ('Southwestern Islands'), which form a 1,100km chain stretching from the major Japanese island of Kyushu to Taiwan's northeast coast. The Nansei Islands are divided into the Satsunan Islands, which make up the northern half of the chain, and the Ryukyu Islands in the south. The latter include the Okinawan Islands and the Sakishima Islands, of which the Senkakus are part (see Map 3).[2]

The islands cover a small area of about 6km$^2$, but this belies their economic and strategic importance. Firstly, they have a bearing on the dispute between Japan and China over their maritime border in the East China Sea. The two countries rely on conflicting provisions of the United Nations Convention on the Law of the Sea (UNCLOS). Japan bases its claim on UNCLOS's normal limit of 200 nautical miles for exclusive economic zones (EEZs) and the UNCLOS principles of 'equidistance' and 'equitable solution'.[3] China bases its claim on the UNCLOS principle of the 'natural prolongation' of the continental shelf, stretching from the Chinese coast out to the 2,000m-deep Okinawa Trough, a distance of 350nm. Since the East China Sea is narrower than 400nm, Tokyo has called for a median line running through the East China Sea. For China, the disputed area lies between Japan's proposed median line and the Okinawa Trough; for Japan, it is area where the two countries' 200nm EEZs would overlap.[4]

According to the US Energy Information Administration, between 60m and 100m barrels of oil in proven and probable reserves and between 1 trillion and 2tr cubic feet in proven and probable natural-gas reserves lie beneath the floor of the East China Sea.[5] Chinese sources claim that undiscovered resources may amount to 70m–160m barrels of oil and up to 250tr cubic feet of gas, mostly in the Xihu and Okinawa troughs.[6]

Secondly, the islands have a strategic significance. Even before the end of the Second World War, the US military sought to build a substantial military presence in the Senkaku/Diaoyu Islands and the other Ryukyus as a bulwark against Soviet expansionism.[7] In 1948, the US Central Intelligence Agency published a top-secret analysis, warning that if the Communists won the civil war in China, the return of the Ryukyus to China would give the Soviet Union access to the islands and endanger the entire US Pacific base system, as well as Japan.[8] The JSDF now plan for a scenario under which China invades the disputed islands; Chinese strategists are reportedly developing plans for a maritime breakout into the Western Pacific that is centred on the Ryukyu Islands, which the US and Japan are committed to defend.[9]

Finally, the islands have a symbolic significance as a result of political choices made by nationalist politicians in Beijing and Tokyo. China regards the 'return' of the Diaoyu Islands as integral to the country's re-emergence. For Japan, retaining the islands confirms that it is still a major power not to be trifled with.

## Histories and controversies

In 1895 Japan claimed the islands as *terra nullius* (unclaimed and uninhabited territory), and has since administered them continuously.[10] China rejects this, tracing its own claim back several centuries. According to one publication, China discovered and named the islands in 1403.[11]

The characterisation of the islands as *terra nullius* in the nineteenth century is one of the most controversial aspects of the dispute. At the time, Meiji Japan was a rising power while China was in decline. Japan insists that its incorporation of the islands was separate from its military victory over China in the 1894–95 Sino-Japanese War and the 1895 Shimonoseki Treaty in which Taiwan and the Pescadore Islands were ceded to Japan by the Qing Dynasty.[12] This is contested by Beijing, which argues that the islands were seized as spoils of war along with Taiwan and all islands appertaining or belonging to it.[13]

The fact that the Japanese government expressed some hesitation in asserting a claim to the Senkaku/Diaoyu Islands in advance of their incorporation in January 1895 has been interpreted by some as showing that Japan at least implicitly admitted to the Qing government's title to the islands.[14] Although the Japanese assert that official surveys of the islands were conducted prior to their incorporation, documents suggest that no such studies took place. According to a May

1894 letter from the Okinawan prefectural governor to the Bureau of Ministry of Home Affairs, there existed no records of the islands or any 'transcribed evidence or folklore and legends demonstrating that the islands' belonged to Japan.[15]

China's claim to prior ownership is undermined by the fact that it did not establish a permanent settlement on the islands, although there are claims that Chinese fishermen used them as places of temporary shelter and repair.[16] Japan, by contrast, has demonstrated effective control over the islands since 1895. Japanese nationals developed and exploited the islands, constructing docks, reservoirs and warehouses as well as collecting bird feathers and guano.[17]

At the end of the Second World War, Japan was compelled to give up the territories it had seized during hostilities. According to China, the Diaoyu Islands should have been placed under Chinese jurisdiction under the provisions of two wartime declarations by the Allied powers.[18] The 1943 Cairo Declaration, which was issued by the United States, the United Kingdom and the Republic of China, stated that the 'Three Great Allies' were bringing 'unrelenting pressure' against Japan to punish its aggression. They agreed that Japan should be 'stripped of all the islands in the Pacific which she has seized or occupied since the beginning of the first World War in 1914'. It also stated that 'all the territories Japan has stolen from the Chinese, such as Manchuria, Formosa, and The Pescadores, shall be restored to the Republic of China', and that Japan be expelled from 'all other territories which she has taken by violence and greed'.[19] The Potsdam Declaration, issued in 1945 by the US, UK and Republic of China (and later 'adhered to' by the Soviet Union), was formally named the Proclamation Defining Terms for Japanese Surrender. It stated that the terms of the Cairo Declaration should be carried out, and that Japan's sovereignty should be limited to the 'islands of Honshu,

Hokkaido, Kyushu, Shikoku and such minor islands' as deter-mined by the three signatories.[20] In signing the surrender document in August 1945, Japan explicitly accepted the terms of the declaration.

Japan would counter that because the islands had come under Japanese control before the signing of the Treaty of Shimonoseki, they should not be included under the purview of the Cairo and Potsdam declarations. Crucially, the treaties that defined Japan's territory after 1945 treated the islands as possessions of Japan prior to the outbreak of hostili-ties.[21] Japan's claim was buttressed by the 1951 San Francisco Treaty which formally made peace between Japan and the Allies. In the treaty, Japan agreed to place under US trustee-ship the Nansei-shoto south of the latitude 29°N, including the Ryukyu and Daito islands.[22] Under Article 3 of the treaty, the US was granted the 'right to exercise all and any powers of administration, legislation and jurisdiction over the terri-tory and inhabitants of these islands, including their territorial waters'.[23] The treaty referred to other islands that had reverted to Chinese control or which China claimed. These included Taiwan (named as Formosa) and the Pescadores, as well as the Spratlys and the Paracels in the South China Sea.[24] However, it did not name the Senkaku/Diaoyu Islands. The decision to merge them into the Ryukyus was made subsequently. As Jean-Marc Blanchard argues, the US military forcefully insisted on grouping *all* islands together and objected to any actions (such as partial reversions) that might endanger this 'monolith' that encompassed the Senkaku/Diaoyu in the Ryukyu chain.[25]

At the San Francisco peace treaty conference, US negotia-tor John Foster Dulles (later secretary of state) stated that the Japanese had 'residual sovereignty' in the Ryukyu Islands. According to an official analysis prepared by the US Army, this meant that 'the United States will not transfer its sovereign powers [administrative, legislative, and jurisdiction] over the Ryukyu Islands to any nation other than Japan'.[26] At the time and thereafter, it was accepted that US control would be transient and that sovereignty over the Ryukus would revert to Japan. Indeed, residual Japanese sovereignty was a prerequisite for the transfer of temporary control to the US. A June 1951 memo prepared by Dulles for a meeting with Secretary of Defense George Marshall clarified this, and added that if Japan were to relinquish sovereignty it might create an opening for either the UN or the Soviets to become involved in the Ryukus.[27]

According to Paul Smith, the rationale for residual sovereignty rested on three pillars. Firstly, the US sought to cultivate Japan as an ally in the Asia-Pacific; its southern islands were viewed as essential elements of the American defensive perimeter. Secondly, the residual-sovereignty formula – and the underlying assumption that it was a precursor to ultimate reversion of sovereignty to Japan – offered the Japanese an incentive to allow the US government maximum flexibility regarding the use of American bases in Okinawa. Lastly, residual sovereignty would assuage anti-American sentiment in Okinawa and mainland Japan at a time when Japan was becoming more assertive.[28] As Smith observes:

> The Senkaku/Diaoyu Islands, as a component of the Ryukyu Island group, were included in this Japanese residual-sovereignty formula, particularly as there was little or no indication that, prior to the late 1960s, the United States sought to disaggregate the Senkaku/Diaoyu Islands and their legal status from that of the overall Ryukyu group. In fact, a US military 'islands monolith' policy ensured that the Senkakus had the same status as that of all the other Ryukyu Islands. In other words, as one scholar has explained,

'the preferences of the U.S. military, then, resulted in the linkage of the Diaoyu [Senkaku] Islands with the Ryukyu Islands and prevented their disassociation from the Ryukyus.'[29]

Thus the Japanese felt encouraged to consider the islands as being included in the residual sovereignty over Okinawa since, for Tokyo, the islands were part of Okinawa.[30]

In 1968 a geophysical survey was conducted under the auspices of the UN Economic Commission for Asia and the Far East (ECAFE), which reported that the continental shelf between Taiwan and Japan might be rich in oil reserves.[31] This invigorated latent claims to the Senkaku/Diaoyu islands on the part of Taipei and Beijing.[32] Around the same time, the US and Japan were negotiating for the formal reversion of the Ryukyu Islands to Japan. Sentiment within Japan was strongly in favour, because of military accidents on the islands, concerns about radioactive containment from US nuclear vessels in the vicinity and disgust with the war in Vietnam.[33] In late 1968, US President Richard Nixon said that reversion was critical to the maintenance of the US–Japan alliance, which he described as the 'linchpin of security in the Pacific'.[34] In November 1969, the two governments issued a joint statement that affirmed reversion within three years was possible without undermining security in the Far East.[35] In June 1971, an agreement on reversion was signed.[36]

That agreement sparked widespread protests in China. In January, more than a thousand Chinese students staged a protest in front of UN Headquarters and the Japanese Consulate-General in New York. In March 1971, more than 500 Chinese scholars and scientists living in the US sent a telegram to Taiwanese President Chiang Kai-shek, urging him to take a firm position against 'new Japanese aggression'.[37] There were similar protests in Hong Kong and Taiwan; the latter, in the view of US officials, had the tacit approval of the Taiwanese authorities.[38] In a meeting with National Security Advisor Henry Kissinger, Ambassador Chow Shu-kai emphasised that the 'final disposition' of the Senkaku/Diaoyu Islands should be kept open. He stressed that the issue was a measure of the Republic of China (ROC)'s ability to 'protect itself', even though the islands were only of 'symbolic importance'.[39]

Taiwan's position on the Senkaku/Diaoyu Islands had been clear and consistent. The ROC did not object to the placement of the Nansei Islands (including the Senkaku/Diaoyu Islands) under American trusteeship, since the arrangement ensured the ROC's survival. Taiwanese acquiescence towards the trusteeship arrangement reflected Cold War considerations, whereby both Taiwan and Japan were allies of the US, arrayed against Communist China. However, to the Taiwanese, the placement of the Nansei Islands under American trusteeship had no connection to the question of sovereignty. It was the opinion of the ROC that the Potsdam and Cairo declarations had already rescinded Japanese sovereignty over the Nansei Islands.[40] Taipei objected to the notion that the 1951 San Francisco Treaty had allowed Japan to retain residual sovereignty over the disputed islands, a position Beijing also took after the PRC took over China's UN membership in 1971.[41]

In the face of pressure from Taiwan, the US adopted a new stance: the dispute between Japan and the ROC (and by extension, the PRC) was a matter to be resolved by the parties involved. This was a clear break from the earlier American position that residual sovereignty rested with Japan. A memorandum prepared by John H. Holdridge of the US National Security Council in April 1971 for Kissinger lays out the competing claims. Holdridge noted the Chinese claim that historical records since the early fifteenth century had considered the

Senkakus/Diaoyus as the boundary separating Taiwan from the independent kingdom of the Ryukyus; that the geological structure of the Senkakus/Diaoyus was similar to other islets associated with Taiwan, and that for 'regional security considerations' Taiwan had not opposed the US occupation of the islands under Article 3 of the 1951 San Francisco Treaty, and that international law holds that military occupation of an area 'does not affect the ultimate determination of sovereignty'. On the other hand, Holdridge observed that the Japanese government had a 'comparable list of apparently offsetting arguments and maintain simply that the Senkakus remain Japanese'. The position of the State Department was that the US 'passes no judgement as to conflicting claims over any portion of them, which should be settled directly by the parties concerned'.[42]

In late October 1971, Beijing took Taipei's seat at the UN and with it the responsibility for upholding the Chinese claim to the islands. At around the same time, Robert Starr, a staff attorney at the US State Department, articulated the new US policy of neutrality regarding the Senkaku/Diaoyu Islands:

> The Governments of the Republic of China and Japan are in disagreement as to sovereignty over the Senkaku Islands. You should know as well that the People's Republic of China has also claimed sovereignty over the islands. The United States believes that a return of administrative rights over those islands to Japan, from which the rights were received, *can in no way prejudice any underlying claims.* The United States cannot add to the legal rights Japan possessed before it transferred administration of the islands to us, nor can the United States, by giving back what it received, diminish the rights of other claimants. The United States *has made no claim to the Senkaku Islands and considers that any*

*conflicting claims to the islands are a matter for resolution by the parties concerned.*[43]

The American volte-face angered Japanese officials, who argued that the retention of US gunnery ranges in the Senkakus/Diaoyus was inconsistent with a policy of neutrality.[44] However, neither China nor Taiwan was convinced by US protestations of neutrality. Kissinger himself was aware of the uncomfortable position in which the US found itself. At the point in Holdridge's text that stated the US 'passes no judgement' on the competing claims, Kissinger wrote: 'But this is nonsense since it gives (the) islands to Japan. How can we get a more neutral position?'[45] Moreover, the US had not only exacerbated the dispute by handing over the islands to Japan, it extended a security guarantee to them, under the terms of the US–Japan alliance. Decades later, the Chinese would argue that such an arrangement constituted 'backroom deals'.[46]

The control of the Senkakus/Diaoyus exercised by Japan since 1972, and underpinned by the US security guarantee, has helped to deter China from seeking to take control of the islands. So too did the shelving arrangements agreed by Japan and China during the 1970s. However, the shelving agreements lapsed with the start of a new century and, for China's leadership, which sees itself as re-establishing the country as a great power and banishing the consequences of the 'Century of Humiliation', the Senkaku/Diaoyu Islands have outsized importance.

## The 'shelving' agreement

Japan's government denies that an understanding was reached between the two states in 1972 to 'shelve' the dispute, thus allowing bilateral relations to develop. However, there is plenty of evidence to support the contention. According to Zhang

Xiangshan, an adviser to Chinese Premier Zhou Enlai, Japanese Prime Minister Kakuei Tanaka had asked Zhou about the islands. In reply, Zhou said that he did not want to 'discuss the issue at this time'. Tanaka pressed further, saying it would be difficult for him if he returned to Japan without mentioning the islands. Zhou replied that 'because oil had been discovered in the ocean there, Taiwan had made (the islands) into a big issue, now the United States is also making them into an issue'.[47] On 25 October 1978, when Chinese Vice Premier Deng Xiaoping visited Japan to ratify the Sino-Japanese Treaty of Peace and Friendship, he told reporters following a meeting with Japanese Prime Minister Takeo Fukuda that both sides had decided 'not to deal' with the issue as they negotiated the treaty:

> It is okay to temporarily shelve such an issue if our generation does not have enough wisdom to resolve it. The next generation will have more wisdom, and I am sure they will eventually find a way acceptable to both sides.[48]

The Chinese position has been expressed clearly and consistently ever since. Speaking to Japanese Prime Minister Yoshihiko Noda at a 15-minute meeting on the sidelines of an Asia-Pacific Economic Cooperation (APEC) gathering in September 2012, Chinese President Hu Jintao said that the two sides had effectively agreed to defer the contentious issue of the disputed islands.[49] Speaking to journalists in October 2012, Chinese Vice Foreign Minister Zhang Zhijun said the consensus by an older generation of Chinese and Japanese leadership for the 'putting aside of the Diaoyu Dao issue' fostered the development of China–Japan relations.[50]

In Diet discussions Japanese officials agreed that it was in Tokyo's interests to go along with Deng's October 1978 proposal to leave things for the next 20 or 30 years. Writing in 1981, Foreign Minister Sunao Sonoda said that it was true that China was claiming the islands as Chinese territory.[51] But the islands were in Japanese hands, and had not become an issue between the two countries. If Japan had taken the trouble to bring up the subject in 1978, it would wake a sleeping dog (literally 'disturb a bush only to let a snake out').[52] This would be a total loss for Japan. In September 1990, a crisis erupted over Japan's preparations to recognise a lighthouse built on Uotsuri/ Diaoyu Dao as a navigational guidepost. This led to an abortive attempt by Taiwanese athletes to plant an Olympic-style torch on the islands and claims to the islands by both Taipei and Beijing. Speaking on 20 October 1990, Misoji Sakamoto, Japan's chief cabinet secretary, reaffirmed Japan's claim to the islands but also cited Deng's 1978 statement that ownership of the islands should be settled by a later generation.[53] After China promulgated its 1992 Law of the People's Republic of China on its Territorial Waters and their Contiguous Waters, which included the Diaoyu Islands, Japanese Prime Minister Kiichi Miyazawa reportedly referred to Japan's prior understanding with Deng over the islands; the Japanese Foreign Ministry later issued a correction, denying the existence of such an arrangement.[54]

There is also extensive evidence of retired or former Japanese officials who had first-hand knowledge of the mutual agreement to defer the territorial dispute. Serving Japanese officials hold to the official position that Tokyo had never agreed to defer the island dispute, while an increasing number of retired politicians and officials have indicated otherwise. In 2012, former vice foreign minister and director general of the Foreign Ministry's Treaties Division Takakazu Kuriyama, who was involved in the Sino-Japanese negotiations in 1972 and 1978, stated that he understood that there was a 'tacit understanding' between the two countries to shelve the territorial dispute.[55] In June 2013, Hiromu Nonaka, a former chief cabinet secretary and a long-time member of the faction once led by Tanaka, confirmed that Japan and China had agreed to shelve the dispute over the islands.[56] His comments drew a quick riposte by Foreign Minister Fumio Kishida, who said there is 'no such fact in our country's diplomatic records'.[57] The most significant remarks came from former prime minister Yukio Hatoyama. Speaking to Hong Kong's Phoenix TV, he said he understood why China thought that Japan had 'stolen' the Senkaku/Diaoyu Islands from China. In stark contrast to the Japanese government's firmly held position that there was no dispute over the islands, Hatoyama called them 'disputed territory'.[58]

## Competing claims

Tokyo and Beijing have built their respective claims by cherry-picking aspects of the historical record. In general, Japan relies on modern notions of international law, while China's case rests on concepts of historical title. As Daqing Yang notes, China attaches great importance to the period of Chinese initial discovery of the islands, whereas Japan stresses its decades of unchallenged administration.[59]

China's claim is based on two main arguments: that the islands were not *terra nullius* in 1895, but rather established Chinese possessions; and that the post-war settlement obliged Japan to return the islands, together with its other war booty, to their rightful owners.

Chinese officials point to references to the islands in documents dating to the Ming Dynasty in the fifteenth century. The Chinese aver that there are many records about Uotsuri/Diaoyu Dao, the largest of the islands, in reports written by Chinese imperial envoys at the time. For example, the Records of the Imperial Title-conferring Envoys to Ryukyu (*Shi Liu Qiu Lu*) written in 1534 by Chen Kan, stated that 'the ship has passed Diaoyu Dao, Huangmao Yu, Chi Yu ... Then Gumi Mountain [Kume Island, in Okinawa Prefecture] comes into sight, that is where the land of Ryukyu begins.'[60] Between the fifteenth and nineteenth centuries, the Ryukyu Kingdom ruled most of the Nansei Islands. The kingdom's first historical record, the 1650 Annals of Chong-shan (*Zhong Shan Shi Jian*), confirmed that Gumi Mountain was part of Ryukyu's territory, while Chi Yu (Chiwei Yu, the smallest and easternmost of the five Senkakus/Diaoyus) and the areas to its west were not. In 1708, Cheng Shunze (Tei Junsoku), a noted scholar and the Grand Master with the Purple-Golden Ribbon (*Zi Jin Da Fu*) of Ryukyu, recorded in his book *A General Guide* (*Zhi Nan Guang Yi*) that 'Gumi Mountain is the mountain guarding the southwest border of Ryukyu'.[61] Gumi Mountain, which the Japanese today call Kumejima (Kume Island), forms part of the Okinawa group of islands which lie at the northeastern corner of the Ryukyu Islands.

China can also point to Japanese sources in support of its claim that it owned the islands prior to 1895. In 1785 a Japanese military scholar, Shihei Hayashi, produced a map on which he gave the islands Chinese names and coloured them pink, the same colour he used for China.[62] Drawing on these and other sources, China argues that the Diaoyu Islands were claimed by and were part of Chinese territory prior to their annexation by Japan in 1895. China also contests the Japanese insistence that surveys were undertaken in the years prior to annexation of the islands.[63]

The second point centres on the contention that the islands were war booty, seized by Japan following the defeat of the Qing government confirmed by the Treaty of Shimonoseki.[64] Thus, China contends, the islands, as part of Taiwan, should have been returned under the terms of the Cairo and Potsdam declarations. [65] China regards the US–Japanese decision on administration of the islands to be illegal but in any case, as Taiwan argued prior to 1971, US administration did not have any bearing on the question of sovereignty. In its arguments, China sometimes relies on a sweeping statement that Japan is challenging the post-war international order by retaining the islands. [66.]

Japan's claim rests, firstly, on the international legal principle of *terra nullius*. According to Japanese authorities, surveys of the Senkaku Islands were conducted prior to their annexation through agencies of the Okinawa Prefecture and other methods. The surveys showed that the islands were not only uninhabited, but also showed no trace of being under the control of China. [67]

Secondly, Japan contends that the islands were not part of Taiwan or the Pescadores which were ceded to Japan under the 1895 Treaty of Shimonoseki. Japan annexed the islands in January 1895, while the treaty was signed in April of that year and came into effect one month later. [68] As a result, the islands are not imperial possessions that Japan was obliged to surrender at the end of the Second World War. The Japanese government points to the fact that the Senkaku Islands were not included with 'Formosa [Taiwan] and the Pescadores' that it renounced under the 1951 San Francisco Treaty. Rather, the Senkakus are regarded as territory that belonged to Japan before its imperial expansion. [69] On that basis, the US was able to exercise administrative rights over the Senkakus as part of the Nansei Islands. [70]

Given that recourse to an adjudicating body such as the International Court of Justice (ICJ) would be based on relatively modern principles of international law (and not historical claims such as China relies on), Japan might appear to have the stronger argument, based on its consistent and unchallenged control over the islands and the failure of successive Chinese governments to claim title to the islands between 1895 and 1971. However, the timing, decision-making process and secrecy of Japan's acquisition of the islands, as well as the transition at the end of the nineteenth century from a Chinese-dominated order in East Asia to one dominated by Western international law, weaken the foundations of Japan's incorporation of the islands.[71]

Even if Japan only formally regained the islands in 1972, successive Chinese governments must have known that Japan controlled the islands and that its citizens had settled there. At the same time, the timing and circumstances of the Chinese claims at the beginning of the 1970s 'cast suspicions' on the motives behind their belated claims, as Zhou Enlai hinted in 1972.[72]

William Heflin, an international lawyer who has provided the most succinct assessment of the respective Chinese and Japanese claims, believes that Japan's is the more persuasive claim. This is because it has exercised sovereign authority over the islands 'peacefully and continuously' since 1972, if not for more than a century.[73] As for China, its inaction in defending its claims – due to the hardship caused by a civil war and nearly 20 years of civil unrest – cannot be considered a valid excuse before the ICJ:

> Therefore, if Japan and China submitted their dispute over the Diaoyu/Senkaku Islands to the ICJ, the adjudicating Chamber of the ICJ would primarily look to the recent historical record of the exercise authority [sic] by each sovereign over the islands. Though inequitable in a historical context, under the current law governing territorial disputes over islands, the

ICJ would likely find that Japan's post-War peaceful exercise of actual authority over the islands had extinguished China's long historical claim.[74]

Although Japan might appear to have the better legal case, it is not prepared to admit there is a dispute that should be taken to arbitration. China, for its part, is determined to resolve the issue without the involvement of third parties. As a result, there is currently no prospect of a negotiated or arbitrated solution.

## Chinese salami slicing

The decline of the shelving agreement and Japan's refusal to acknowledge a dispute exists has encouraged China to press its claims directly, by actions aimed at eroding Japan's effective administration over the islands. Within China, there is a widely held belief that Japan could cement its de facto control of the islands if its control regime runs unchallenged for 50 years from 1972 (when the US returned control to Japan), based on the legal doctrine of 'acquisition prescription'.[75] Through their incursions into the Senkaku/Diaoyu Islands, the Chinese are seeking to change the facts on the ground. In September 2012, for example, four vessels from the Chinese State Oceanic Administration sought to chase Japanese ships out of the waters surrounding the disputed islands.[76]

The trend of challenging Japan's de facto control of the islands started as early as 2004, when seven Chinese activists landed on Uotsuri/Diaoyu Dao. For the first time, the Japanese police made arrests under Japan's immigration management law, which includes a clause on expulsion of illegal foreign trespassers.[77] The Chinese Foreign Ministry protested, calling it a serious breach of sovereignty. The central government then reportedly intervened at the last minute, did not press for an indictment and ordered the release of the arrested Chinese.

Apparently, Tokyo did not want to imperil the upcoming visit by Foreign Minister Yoriko Kawaguchi to China.[78] At that point, it was still reasonable to expect an implicit adherence to the 1970s-era shelving agreement by both China and Japan. The Japanese reportedly told the Chinese that future protesters would not be detained, only arrested, so long as it was not a serious case; in turn, the Chinese promised the Japanese that they would seek to prevent protesters from leaving Chinese harbours. Unsurprisingly, such an understanding was denied by both governments.[79]

In February 2007, the JCG detected a Chinese research ship in the vicinity of the Senkaku Islands and warned it to stop operations. The ship refused and the Japanese government protested, on the grounds that under UNCLOS, foreign survey or research activities were not permitted without Tokyo's permission. Beijing replied that notification was not needed since the Diaoyu Islands were part of Chinese territory.[80] The situation deteriorated in 2008, when the JCG spotted two ships of the China Marine Surveillance (CMS) force in the Senkaku/Diaoyu Islands area. The operation was well planned. The ships left Shanghai and Ningbo to rendezvous in the East China Sea. This was interpreted by Japan as a major escalation by the Chinese, going beyond previous cases of intrusion by fishermen or protesters.[81] In China, the 'twin heroes' of the operation were feted. In comments underscoring the Chinese proclivity for challenging behaviour, CMS Deputy Director Sun Shuxian declared that 'in sea areas where there is a territorial dispute under international law, it is important to display presence in the sea area under jurisdiction and continue accumulating records of effective control'. In other words, the more China maintains a presence in what Japan claims as its territorial waters, the stronger is China's claim to the disputed islands.[82]

The September 2010 arrest of the Chinese trawler captain near the islands raised the temperature still further. The trawler was operating very close to the islands when challenged by the JCG; he responded by attempting to ram two coast-guard vessels and was subsequently detained and charged under Japanese law. His crew was released six days later but the captain spent a further week in detention. As one Japanese analyst noted, the charging of the captain under domestic law led to a 'combination of unfortunate elements' that caused the biggest crisis in Sino-Japanese relations since the 2005 anti-Japanese protests in China over Tokyo's handling of its wartime history.[83] Partly this was because Japan treated it as a straightforward legal matter, which infuriated the Chinese. The captain was charged for 'obstruction in the execution of public duty' (*koumu shikkou bougai*).[84] This seemed to signal a departure from Japan's past handling of the dispute. In 2004, for example, Tokyo arrested individuals who travelled to the disputed islands but deported them quickly without charge, allowing tensions to dissipate quickly.[85] As Prime Minister Naoto Kan challenged Ichiro Ozawa for the leadership of the Democratic Party of Japan (DPJ), he delegated the handling of the matter to Yoshito Sengoku, the chief cabinet secretary, and Seiji Maehara, the land, infrastructure, transport and tourism minister. Both men stated their intent to 'solemnly handle this matter according to the domestic law' (*shukushuku to kokunai-hou wo tekiyou suru*) and that 'there is no territorial problem' (*ryodo mondai wasonzai shinai*). The parsing of such terms left little room for discretion and manoeuvre in the tense stand-off with China.[86]

Japan's response surprised Beijing, which expected more sensitivity from a DPJ government. Chinese decision-makers were taken aback by Japan's assertion of its sovereignty over the disputed islands through the application of domestic legislation, which marked a departure from the tacit understanding to shelve the dispute.[87] To Wang Xiangsui, the director of the Center for Security Strategy at the Beijing University of Aeronautics and Astronautics, Japan was trying to get China to eat the 'bitter fruit' of its sovereignty over the islands. They want China to 'accept the fact that they control the islands'.[88] In retaliation, China suspended exports of rare earths to Japan, cancelled a second round of talks about a 2008 understanding on energy cooperation in the East China Sea and postponed the visit of 1,000 Japanese youth to the Shanghai World Exhibition, which had been planned for the period from 21 September.[89]

The true turning point in the dispute occurred in September 2012, when the Japanese government announced that it would purchase the leases for three of the five islands from their private owners, who bought Kitakojima and Minamikojima in 1972 and Uotsuri/Diaoyu Dao in 1978 from their previous private owners. The decision by the Noda government was ostensibly to pre-empt the purchase of the islands by Shintaro Ishihara, the right-wing governor of Tokyo, so that the islands would be 'administered peacefully and stably'.[90] Throughout the subsequent crisis, the Noda government maintained that the transaction was a commercial one which had changed ownership of the islands from private to public hands. Noda also reasoned that the purchase should be completed before the start of the new Chinese administration of president-in-waiting Xi Jinping.[91] Foreign Minister Koichiro Gemba wrote that the purchase merely signified the reversion of title back to Tokyo, a status of affairs that had been sustained until 1932. Moreover, the purchase was meant to minimise any 'adverse impact' on Sino-Japanese relations.[92] China protested vehemently, and anti-Japanese protests broke out across the country.

Misunderstandings and mutual suspicion exacerbated matters. Japan's government used the term 'nationalisation' in a technical sense, of ownership of an asset switching from private to government control. To many Chinese, however, the term implied that Japan was strengthening its claim on the islands, in effect occupying or seizing Chinese territory.[93] From the onset, the Chinese government rejected Tokyo's rationale for the purchase, saying that it would change the status quo. At the APEC summit in Vladivostok on 9 September, Hu Jintao told Noda that Japan's decision to purchase the islands was 'illegal' and 'invalid'. Noda's subsequent announcement, two days later, about the completion of the purchase was perceived to be insulting and insensitive to China. In addition, the crisis happened in the run-up to the 18th National Congress of the Chinese Communist Party. On 15–16 September, an estimated 1.5m people protested in more than 100 cities across China.[94] To the Chinese, Japan's rationale for nationalisation, couched as it was as a pre-emptive move aimed at preventing Ishihara from carrying out actions that would imperil Sino-Japanese relations, was a ruse. To them, the purchase was a Japanese ploy to present Beijing with a fait accompli.[95] To Zhang Zhijun, Japan's attempt to present China with two choices – nationalisation or the purchase of the islands by Ishihara – was akin to choosing between 'two kinds of poison'.[96]

Beijing hit back with economic sanctions and a consumer boycott of Japanese goods, as well as an escalation of its efforts to challenge and erode Japanese control over the islands. On 10 September, the Chinese government announced the base points and baselines of the territorial waters of the disputed islands and their affiliated islets. On 21 September, China deposited with the United Nations a list of these coordinates for the islands – a move that met with Japanese protests three days later. In the military dimension, a raft of maritime and aerial incursions into the vicinity of the disputed islands occurred. By 17 May 2013, CMS and Fisheries Law Enforcement Command

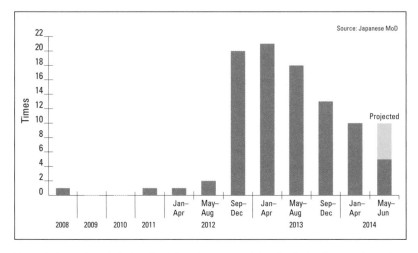

Figure 1: **Incursions into territorial waters around the Senkaku/Diaoyu Islands by Chinese government ships**

vessels had entered the territorial waters of the disputed islands for the 45th time since the nationalisation announcement the previous September.[97] By 18 July the figure had risen to 52 (see Figure 1).[98]

In December 2012, the Chinese sought to erode or at the least discredit Japanese claims of control over the islands. On 13 December 2012, a small Y-12 turboprop aircraft of the CMS entered airspace over the disputed islands. This marked the first such breach of Japanese-claimed airspace since 1958, when the Japan Air Self Defense Force (JASDF) started collecting data (see Figure 2).[99] Chief Cabinet Secretary Osamu Fujimura said the intrusion constituted another bid by China to claim control over the islands.[100] In early January 2013, the PLA Air Force (PLAAF) scrambled two J-10 fighters to the East China Sea, after a Y-8 aircraft was reported to have been tailed by two JASDF F-15 fighters as it patrolled airspace southwest of an oil platform.[101] An even more serious incident occurred on 30 January 2013, when a Chinese frigate allegedly locked weapons-guiding radars on a Japanese navy ship near the disputed

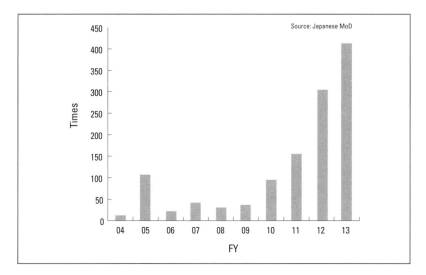

Figure 2: **Japanese aircraft scrambles against Chinese aircraft, FY 2004–2013**

islands.[102] Chinese officials strenuously denied that such a 'lock on' occurred, but a former Japanese official said that the incident put the two countries 'precariously close to exchanging fire for the first time' in the post-war era.[103] In September 2013, China deployed an unmanned drone near the Senkaku/Diaoyu Islands, and Japan announced it would consider shooting down the aircraft if Japanese airspace were violated. China countered by saying that shooting down the drone would constitute 'an act of war' and that it would take 'decisive action to strike back'. The tensions coincided with China's first public display of its nuclear submarine force, underscoring China's growing confidence.[104]

On 23 November 2013, China took its challenging strategy a step further by declaring an Air Defence Identification Zone (ADIZ) covering part of the East China Sea and the Senkaku/Diaoyu Islands (see Map 4). The ADIZ overlapped with the ADIZs of Japan, South Korea and Taiwan. China justified the setting up of the ADIZ as a 'justified act of self-defence' and not aimed at any specific country. China's Ministry of

National Defence said that any aircraft would have to notify the Chinese authorities in advance and follow the instructions from the administrative organ of the East China Sea ADIZ. China's military would adopt 'defensive emergency measures' if aircraft failed to cooperate.[105] A Foreign Ministry spokesman said that 'relevant countries' need not make a 'fuss' about the zone.[106] China said that the setting up of the zone was in line with other ADIZs set up by more than 20 other countries, including the United States, Japan and South Korea.[107]

The ADIZ drew strong reactions. On 26 November, the US sent two unarmed B-52s from Guam into the ADIZ without notification. The flight took place without incident and highlighted the fact that the Chinese were either unwilling or unable to enforce the ADIZ.[108] China's establishment of the ADIZ attracted opprobrium from many quarters, including South Korea and Japan – two allies of the US which were also involved in a mutual diplomatic impasse due to Seoul's perceptions that Japan was not taking historical issues seriously. Even Australia, which had traditionally been supportive of China's rise to great-power status, signed a communiqué at the November 2013 Trilateral Strategic Dialogue between Australia, Japan and the US that stated opposition to 'any coercive and unilateral actions that could change the status quo in the East China Sea'. The language mirrored that of the US, which had warned China against changing the status quo in the Asia-Pacific.[109] More importantly, China's laying down of the ADIZ eroded the goodwill that it had built up with its oft-repeated notions of the country's 'peaceful rise' and damaged the efforts that Beijing had put in in late 2013 to reassure its neighbours – especially the ASEAN countries – of its benevolent intentions.[110]

However, the ADIZ both promoted China's claim to the Diaoyu Islands and challenged Japan's effective control. The declaration confirmed that the Diaoyu Islands are a 'core concern' for China – and put the islands in the same category as the South China Sea and Taiwan.[111] According to *Asia Weekly*, a Hong Kong-based publication which often carries reliable reports on foreign-policy deliberations in Beijing, the imposition of the ADIZ was seen as a 'great air–sea strategic breakthrough for China'.[112] In setting up the zone, Chinese President Xi Jinping was not only setting his sights on the Diaoyu Islands but also on the Western Pacific. In signalling his approval for the plan, Xi had reportedly indicated that the move turned 'a contention over resources into a contest in strategies'. Given that China's ADIZ runs close to the strategic Miyako Strait, it would enable the PLA Navy (PLAN) to break the perceived 'encirclement' of China by the US and its allies, by going through the First Island Chain and into the Pacific (see Map 2).[113] The need to break this perceived encirclement was envisioned in the 1980s by Admiral Liu Huaqing in his 'near seas strategy' – and underscored by the PLAN's *Maneuver-5* exercise in October 2013. Chinese analysts also noted that China's top foreign-policy makers believed that the new ADIZ would constitute 'another way to force Japan to recognize that there is a dispute' over the islands.[114] The fashion in which the ADIZ was imposed was also consistent with China's strategic behaviour through history. In the past 60 years or so, whenever Beijing perceived major threats to its core interests, it has sought to deter its adversaries by signalling its preparedness to go to war to protect those interests. It has done so in several instances – the Korean War in 1950, the China–India war in 1962, the Chinese support for North Vietnam in 1965–73 and the Chinese invasion of Vietnam in 1979.[115] The establishment of the ADIZ in November 2013 could be interpreted as falling within the established historical pattern.

The Chinese ADIZ could also be construed as part of a carefully calibrated strategy to test America's commitment to defending the Senkakus/Diaoyus, within the framework of the US–Japan alliance. This would be consistent with the long-term Chinese goal of driving a wedge between the US and Japan over the islands. Compared to ADIZs established by other countries, China's ADIZ has an onerous condition: aircraft must file notifications with the Chinese authorities even if they are not headed towards Chinese airspace.[116] Subsequent actions by the Americans – the B-52 flights into the ADIZ and an emphasis that the islands fall under the aegis of the US–Japan alliance – established their resolve, and sought to signal to the Chinese Washington's commitment to the islands. This had not been apparent earlier in the year, when America hesitated to take sides in the dispute, on the pretext that Japanese officials had made nationalist gestures that antagonised China.[117]

In the absence of crisis-management mechanisms, the risk of conflict was appreciable.[118] One Chinese analyst suggested that China had anticipated that American aircraft would trespass China's ADIZ, and that China would 'probably reciprocate' by sending aircraft through the ADIZs of the US and Japan.[119] Speaking to the *Financial Times*, William Fallon, a former chief of US Pacific Command, said that China's scrambling of jets to intercept aircraft entering its ADIZ would be 'another stick in the fire' and provide an opportunity for 'people to screw up'.[120]

But if the Chinese were looking for a signal from the US that Washington did not intend to escalate the dispute further and thus imperil Sino-American relations, they soon got one. On 28 November, the Chinese sent fighter jets and early-warning aircraft into the ADIZ. A Defence Ministry spokesman said that it was incorrect to assume that China would shoot down any planes that veered into the ADIZ, saying that the 'specific measures' to be taken would be 'decided based on the specific situation and the extent of the threat being faced at the time'.[121] On 29 November, Washington still insisted that it did not accept China's requirement for the ADIZ, but changed its tone by urging American carriers to comply with the ADIZ to ensure the safety of their commercial flights. The move went down badly in Tokyo, particularly after the Japanese government forced Japanese airlines to reverse course after they started providing China with flight plans for the ADIZ.[122] Chinese media was quick to note America's 'softened gesture following the provocative challenge of sending two bombers' into the ADIZ. The nationalist *Global Times* said Washington's guidance to its carriers signalled a 'pragmatic subtle shift of the US stance'.[123] The diplomatic manoeuvres between China and the US established boundary markers for future behaviour, and suggested an informal understanding between the two powers: China used the ADIZ to promote its claim to the islands but would not necessarily enforce the ADIZ; the US would not recognise the ADIZ as binding but encouraged its airlines to observe it, signalling in the process its desire to avoid incidents in the airspace of the East China Sea. This is consistent with Sino-American strategic interactions through history, whereby both parties practised implicit signalling to prevent the risk of escalation. During the Vietnam War in the 1960s, both China and America sought to limit the danger of escalation, having learnt the lessons of abject deterrence failures in the run-up to the Korean War of 1950. In the 1995–96 Taiwan Strait crises, both China and America sought to deter Taiwanese moves towards independence and expended much effort to put their relationship back on a firm strategic footing.[124]

## Notes

1   Richard C. Bush, *Perils of Proximity: China–Japan Security Relations* (Washington DC: Brookings Institution Press, 2010), loc. 954 (Kindle edition).

2   Eric Sayers, 'The "Consequent Interest" of Japan's Southwestern Islands: A Mahanian Appraisal of the Ryukyu Archipelago', *Naval War College Review*, vol. 66, no. 2, Spring 2013, pp. 46–7.

3   Bush, *Perils of Proximity*, loc. 918 (Kindle edition).

4   Reinhard Drifte, 'Territorial Conflicts in the East China Sea: From Missed Opportunities to Negotiation Stalemate', *Asia Pacific Journal*, vol. 22, no. 3, June 2009, http://www.japanfocus.org/-Reinhard-Drifte/3156; Reinhard Drifte, 'From "Sea of Confrontation" to "Sea of Peace, Cooperation and Friendship?" – Japan Facing China in the East China Sea', *Japan Aktuell*, March 2008, p. 31.

5   US Energy Information Administration, 'East China Sea', Analysis Brief, 25 September 2012, http://www.eia.gov/countries/analysisbriefs/east_china_sea/east_china_sea.pdf.

6   *Ibid.*

7   Jean-Marc F. Blanchard, 'The U.S. Role in the Sino-Japanese Dispute over the Diaoyu (Senkaku) Islands, 1945–1971', *China Quarterly*, no. 161, March 2000, p. 104.

8   Ibid., p. 105.

9   Aurelia George Mulgan, 'A Sea of Trouble in Sino-Japanese Relations', *East Asia Forum*, 28 September 2010, http://www.eastasiaforum.org/2010/09/28/a-sea-of-trouble-in-sino-japanese-relations/.

10  Mark E. Manyin, *Senkaku (Diaoyu/Diaoyutai) Islands Dispute: U.S. Treaty Obligations*, CRS Report for Congress R42761 (Washington DC: Congressional Research Service, 22 January 2013), p. 3; Ministry of Foreign Affairs of Japan, 'Fact Sheet on the Senkaku Islands', November 2012, http://www.mofa.go.jp/region/asia-paci/senkaku/fact_sheet.html.

11  *Zhongguo zhoubian guanxi yu anquan huanjing* (China's Relations with Its Neighbours and Its Security Environment) (Shaanxi: People's Education Press, n.d.), in *Joint Publications Research Report* JPRS-China-93-O37, 8 June 1993, pp. 25–6, cited in Blanchard, 'The U.S. Role in the Sino-Japanese Dispute over the Diaoyu (Senkaku) Islands'; State Council Information Office (China), 'Diaoyu Dao, an Inherent Territory of China', White Paper, 25 September 2012, available at http://www.gov.cn/english/official/2012-09/25/content_2232763.htm.

12  Ministry of Foreign Affairs of Japan, 'Fact Sheet on the Senkaku Islands'.

13  State Council Information Office (China), 'Diaoyu Dao, an Inherent Territory of China'.

14  Reinhard Drifte, *The Senkaku/Diaoyu Islands Territorial Dispute between Japan and China: Between the Materialization of the 'China Threat' And Japan 'Reversing The Outcome Of World War II'?*, UNISCI Discussion Papers no. 32 (Madrid: UNISCI, May 2013).

15  Drifte, *The Senkaku/Diaoyu Islands Territorial Dispute*. See also Han-Yi

Shaw, *The Diaoyutai/Senkaku Islands Dispute: Its History and an Analysis of the Ownership Claims of the P.R.C., the R.O.C. and Japan*, Occasional Papers/Reprints Series in Contemporary Asian Studies (Baltimore, MD: University of Maryland, 1999), pp. 83–4.

16  Manyin, *Senkaku (Diaoyu/ Diaoyutai) Islands Dispute*, p. 2.

17  Blanchard, 'The U.S. Role in the Sino-Japanese Dispute over the Diaoyu (Senkaku) Islands', p. 102; Robert H. Wade, 'China–Japan Island Dispute: The Other Side of the Story', *Economic and Political Weekly*, vol. 47, no. 10, 9 March 2013, pp. 27–31.

18  Zhongqi Pan, 'Sino-Japanese Dispute over the Diaoyu/Senkaku Islands: The Pending Controversy from the Chinese Perspective', *Journal of Chinese Political Science*, vol. 12, no. 1, June 2007, p. 82.

19  Text of 1943 Cairo Communiqué, available at National Diet Library (Japan) website, http://www.ndl.go.jp/constitution/e/shiryo/01/002_46/002_46tx.html.

20  Text of 1945 Potsdam Declaration, available at National Diet Library (Japan), http://www.ndl.go.jp/constitution/e/etc/c06.html.

21  Ministry of Foreign Affairs of Japan, 'Fact Sheet on the Senkaku Islands'.

22  Treaty of Peace with Japan, 8 September 1951, available at http://www.taiwandocuments.org/sanfrancisco01.htm.

23  Treaty of Peace with Japan, 8 September 1951.

24  Manyin, *Senkaku (Diaoyu/ Diaoyutai) Islands Dispute*, p. 3.

25  Blanchard, 'The U.S. Role in the Sino-Japanese Dispute over the Diaoyu (Senkaku) Islands', p. 121.

26  *Ibid.* p. 109.

27  'Memorandum by the Consultant to the Secretary (Dulles)', 27 June 1951, in *Foreign Relations of the United States, 1951: Asia and the Pacific*, vol. 6, part 1 (Washington DC: US Government Printing Office, 1951), pp. 1152–3; Blanchard, 'The U.S. Role in the Sino-Japanese Dispute over the Diaoyu (Senkaku) Islands', p. 110.

28  Paul J. Smith, 'The Senkaku/ Diaoyu Island Controversy: A Crisis Postponed', *Naval War College Review*, vol. 66, no. 2, Spring 2013, p. 30.

29  *Ibid.* Smith quotes Blanchard when he used the term 'islands monolith', which refers to the American disposition to ensure that Senkakus had the same legal status as the other Ryukyu Island. See Blanchard, 'The U.S. Role in the Sino-Japanese Dispute over the Diaoyu (Senkaku) Islands', p. 121.

30  Drifte, *The Senkaku/Diaoyu Islands Territorial Dispute*, p. 16.

31  Drifte, 'From "Sea of Confrontation" to "Sea of Peace, Cooperation and Friendship?"', p. 30.

32  Smith, 'The Senkaku/ Diaoyu Island Controversy', p. 31.

33  Blanchard, 'The U.S. Role in the Sino-Japanese Dispute over the Diaoyu (Senkaku) Islands', p. 119.

34  Smith, 'The Senkaku/ Diaoyu Island Controversy', p. 31.

35  Joint Statement by President Nixon and Prime Minister Eisaku Sato, Washington DC, 21 November 1969, available at http://www.niraikanai.wwma.net/pages/archive/sato69.html.

36  Blanchard, 'The U.S. Role in the Sino-Japanese Dispute over the Diaoyu (Senkaku) Islands', p. 119.

37   Frank Ching, 'U.S. Chinese Ask Backing on Isles', *New York Times*, 12 April 1971, cited in Smith, 'The Senkaku/ Diaoyu Island Controversy', p. 32.

38   'Memorandum of Conversation between Ambassador Chow Shu-Kai and Henry A. Kissinger', *Foreign Relations of the United States, 1969–1976*, vol. 17, *China, 1969–1972*, Document 113, note 6, http://history.state.gov/historicaldocuments/frus1969-76v17/d113#fn6.

39   *Ibid.*

40   Shaw, *The Diaoyutai/Senkaku Islands Dispute*, p. 114, n. 135.

41   *Ibid.*

42   'Memorandum From John H. Holdridge of the National Security Council Staff to the President's Assistant for National Security Affairs (Kissinger), Washington, 13 April 1971', *Foreign Relations of the United States, 1969–1976*, vol. 17, *China, 1969–1972*, Document 115, http://history.state.gov/historical documents/frus1969-76v17/d115.

43   Emphasis added. Quoted in Manyin, *Senkaku (Diaoyu/ Diaoyutai) Islands Dispute*, p. 5.

44   Smith, 'The Senkaku/ Diaoyu Island Controversy', p. 36.

45   'Memorandum From John H. Holdridge of the National Security Council Staff to the President's Assistant for National Security Affairs (Kissinger)'.

46   State Council Information Office (China), 'Diaoyu Dao, an Inherent Territory of China'.

47   Cited in M. Taylor Fravel, 'Something to Talk About, Again', *The Diplomat*, 10 October 2012, http://thediplomat.com/china-power/something-to-talk-about-again/.

48   M. Taylor Fravel, 'Explaining Stability in the Senkaku (Diaoyu) Dispute', in Gerald Curtis, Ryosei Kokubun and Wang Jisi (eds), *Getting the Triangle Straight: Managing China–Japan–US Relations* (Washington DC: The Brookings Institution Press, 2010), p. 157. See also 'Evidence Shows Diaoyu Dao is China's Territory', *China Daily*, 15 October 2012, http://www.chinadaily.com.cn/cndy/2012-10/15/content_15816406.htm.

49   'China-watcher Yabuki says Senkakus are a Diplomatic Mistake by Japan', *Asahi Shimbun*, 12 December 2012.

50   See 'Vice Foreign Minister Zhang Zhijun Gave Briefing to Chinese and Foreign Journalists on the Diaoyu Dao Issue (Transcript)', 27 October 2012, http://www.fmprc.gov.cn/eng/topics/diaodao/t983015.shtml. For the original Chinese version, see http://www.fmprc.gov.cn/mfa_chn/zyxw_602251/t982822.shtml.

51   Drifte, *The Senkaku/Diaoyu Islands Territorial Dispute*, p. 20.

52   *Ibid.*

53   Kwan Weng Kin, 'Japanese Government Firm but Restrained in Handling Dispute', *Straits Times*, 2 November 1990; Eric Strecker Downs and Phillip C. Saunders, 'Legitimacy and the Limits of Nationalism: China and the Diaoyu Islands', *International Security*, vol. 23, no. 3, Winter 1998, p. 129.

54   Reinhard Drifte, 'Japanese–Chinese Territorial Disputes in the East China Sea – Between Military Confrontation and Economic Cooperation', working paper, Asia

Research Centre, London School of Economics and Political Science, 2008, p. 5.

55 Susumu Yabuki, 'Sasae gaimu jikan to Kuriyama Takakazu moto gaimu jikan no sekinin wo tou', 6 November 2012, http://www.21ccs.jp/china_watching/DirectorsWatching_YABUKI/Directors_watching_72.html, cited in Drifte, *The Senkaku/Diaoyu Islands Territorial Dispute*, pp. 20–1.

56 Nozomu Hayashi, 'Former LDP Elder: Kakuei Tanaka Said Senkaku Issue Shelved in 1972', *Asahi Shimbun*, 4 June 2013; 'Senkaku Row Shelved in '70s: Nonaka', *Japan Times*, 5 June 2013.

57 'Nonaka Remarks Riled the Senkaku Waters', *Japan Times*, 12 June 2013.

58 Toko Sekiguichi, 'Ex-Japan PM Hatoyama Draws Ire at Home', *Wall Street Journal Online*, 26 June 2013.

59 Daqing Yang, 'History: From Dispute to Dialogue', in Tatsushu Arai, Shihoko Goto and Zheng Wang (eds), *Clash of National Identities: China, Japan and the East China Sea Territorial Dispute* (Washington DC: Woodrow Wilson International Center, 2013), p. 23.

60 State Council Information Office (China), 'Diaoyu Dao, an Inherent Territory of China'.

61 *Ibid.*

62 'Behind the Row over a Bunch of Pacific Rocks Lies the Sad, Magical History of Okinawa', *The Economist*, 22 December 2012.

63 Shaw, *The Diaoyutai/Senkaku Islands Dispute*, pp. 83–4.

64 Bush, *Perils of Proximity*, loc. 962 (Kindle edition).

65 *Ibid.*

66 State Council Information Office (China), 'Diaoyu Dao, an Inherent Territory of China'.

67 Ministry of Foreign Affairs of Japan, 'Fact Sheet on the Senkaku Islands'.

68 *Ibid.*

69 *Ibid.*

70 *Ibid.*

71 Drifte, *The Senkaku/Diaoyu Islands Territorial Dispute*, pp. 58–9.

72 See *ibid.*

73 William B. Heflin, 'Diaoyu/Senkaku Island Dispute, Japan and China: Oceans Apart', *Asia-Pacific Law & Policy Journal*, vol. 1, no. 2, 2000, p. 20.

74 *Ibid.*, pp. 21–2.

75 International Crisis Group, *Dangerous Waters: China–Japan Relations on the Rocks*, Asia Report no. 245 (Brussels: ICG, 8 April 2013), p. 14. Heflin argues that the 1952 treaty between Japan and Taiwan (the Sino-Japanese Treaty), which rendered the Shimonoseki Treaty null and void, thus returned the islands to the Chinese. However, after 1952 Japan jointly administered the islands with the US. Consequently, the safest date to establish from which Japan began to exercise peaceful and continuous sovereign authority over the islands is 1952. See Heflin, 'Diaoyu/Senkaku Island Dispute: Japan and China, Oceans Apart', p. 21, n. 123.

76 David Lague, 'China Navy Seeks To "Wear Out" Japanese Ships In Disputed Waters', Reuters, 6 March 2013; Kathrin Hille and Michiyo Nakamoto, 'China Raises Stakes Over Disputed Islands', *Financial Times*, 30 October 2012, http://www.ft.com/cms/s/0/7d97be3e-

227e-11e2-8edf-00144feabdc0.
html#axzz2NELjM284.

77 Drifte, *The Senkaku/Diaoyu Islands Territorial Dispute*, p. 29. Drifte cites information about the application of the immigration law based on an e-mail from Professor Akio Takahara. See also 'Chinese Activists' Campaigns for Diaoyu Islands', *Beijing Review*, 20 August 2012.

78 Drifte, *The Senkaku/Diaoyu Islands Territorial Dispute*, p. 29.

79 *Ibid.*, pp. 29–30.

80 Bush, *Perils of Proximity*, loc. 984 (Kindle edition).

81 Drifte, *The Senkaku/Diaoyu Islands Territorial Dispute*, pp. 26, 30; Bush, *Perils of Proximity*, loc. 992 (Kindle edition).

82 Bush, *Perils of Proximity*, loc. 1005 (Kindle edition).

83 International Crisis Group, *Dangerous Waters*, p. 20.

84 Shinji Fujihira, 'Can Japanese Democracy Cope with China's Rise?', in Arai, Goto and Wang (eds), *Clash of National Identities*, pp. 40–1.

85 International Crisis Group, *Dangerous Waters*, p. 20; Drifte, *The Senkaku/Diaoyu Islands Territorial Dispute*, p. 32; interview in Tokyo, September 2013.

86 Fujihira, 'Can Japanese Democracy Cope with China's Rise?', pp. 40–1.

87 Drifte, *The Senkaku/Diaoyu Islands Territorial Dispute*, p. 30.

88 Martin Fackler and Ian Johnson, 'Arrest in Disputed Seas Riles China and Japan', *New York Times*, 20 September 2010. It is still debatable whether China had suspended rare-earth exports to China as a result of the September 2010 arrest of the trawler captain. Some analysts argue that China had already planned a general reduction of rare-earth exports as early as August 2010. See Amy King and Shiro Armstrong, 'Did China Really Ban Rare Earth Metal Exports to Japan', *East Asia Forum*, 18 August 2013, http://www.eastasiaforum.org/2013/08/18/did-china-really-ban-rare-earth-metals-exports-to-japan/; Alastair Iain Johnston, 'How New and Assertive is China's New Assertiveness?', *International Security*, vol. 37, no. 4, Spring 2013, pp. 23–6.

89 Drifte, *The Senkaku/Diaoyu Islands Territorial Dispute*, pp. 31–2.

90 Yu Tamura and Seima Oki, 'Senkaku Talks with China End in Stalemate', *Yomiuri Shimbun*, 13 July 2012, http://www.asianewsnet.net/news-33353.html.

91 Fujihira, 'Can Japanese Democracy Cope with China's Rise?', pp. 42–3.

92 Koichiro Genba, 'China–Japan Relations at a Crossroads', *New York Times*, 20 November 2012.

93 Chen Yo-Jung, 'Sino-Japan Ties: Lost in Translation', *Straits Times*, 25 September 2012; interviews in Beijing, August 2013.

94 Fujihira, 'Can Japanese Democracy Cope with China's Rise?', p. 43.

95 Interviews in Beijing, August 2013.

96 'Vice Foreign Minister Zhang Zhijun Gave Briefing to Chinese and Foreign Journalists on the Diaoyu Dao Issue (Transcript)'.

97 '3 Chinese Vessels Enter Japanese Waters Near Senkakus', *Kyodo News*, 17 May 2013.

98 '3 Chinese Vessels Enter Japanese Waters Around Senkakus', *Kyodo News*, 18 July 2013.

99 'Senkaku Air Intrusion Prompts Radar Upgrade', *Japan Times*, 15 December 2012.

100 *Ibid.*

101 'China Sends Fighters to Counter Japanese Aircraft', Xinhua, 11 January 2013.

102 'The Dangerous Dance Around Disputed Islets Is Becoming Ever More Worrying', *The Economist*, 9 February 2013; Martin Fackler, 'Japan Says China Aimed Radar at Ship', *New York Times*, 5 February 2013.

103 Hitoshi Tanaka, 'The Senkaku Islands and Japan–China Relations', *East Asia Forum*, 19 March 2013, http://www.eastasiaforum. org/2013/03/19/the-senkaku-islands-and-japan-china-relations/.

104 Demetri Sevastopulo, 'China–Japan Relations Take Turn for Worse', *Financial Times*, 28 October 2013.

105 'Air Defense Identification Zone of the P.R.C.', Xinhua, 23 November 2013.

106 'No Need to Make a Fuss about China's ADIZ: FM Spokesman', Xinhua, 27 November 2013.

107 'Background: Defense Identification Zones', Xinhua, 24 November 2013.

108 Richard A. Bitzinger, 'Air Defence Zone a "Lose–Lose" for Beijing?', *Straits Times*, 29 November 2013; see also 'U.S. B-52 Bombers Challenge Disputed China Air Zone', BBC, 26 November 2013.

109 Graeme Dobell, 'Haunting AUSMIN', The Strategist, Australian Strategy Policy Institute blog, 29 November 2013, http:// www.aspistrategist.org.au/ haunting-ausmin/.

110 'Crossing a Line in the Sky', *The Economist*, 30 November 2013; Benjamin Schreer, 'Peaceful Rise, Anyone? China's East China Sea Air Defence Identification Zone', The Strategist, Australian Strategy Policy Institute blog, 28 November 2013, http://www.aspistrategist. org.au/peaceful-rise-anyone-chinas-east-china-sea-air-defence-identification-zone/.

111 Alex Neill, 'Why China Air Zone Raises Risk', BBC News, 26 November 2013, http://www.bbc. co.uk/news/world-asia-25086345. See also Harry White, 'The ADIZ and Rebalancing on the Run', The Strategist, Australian Strategy Policy Institute blog, 28 November 2013, http://www.aspistrategist.org. au/the-adiz-and-rebalancing-on-the-run/.

112 'Zhongguo haikong zhanlue tupo fangkong shibie qu juece beihou' (The Basis for China's Air–Sea Strategic Breakthrough using the ADIZ), *Yazhou zhoukan*, (Asia Weekly), 8 December 2013, http:// yzzk.com/cfm/content_archive. cfm?id=1385609654405&docis sue=2013-48; 'New Air Defence Zone "Opens Doorway to Pacific"', *Straits Times*, 4 December 2013.

113 'Zhongguo haikong zhanlue tupo fangkong shibie qu juece beihou'; 'New Air Defence Zone "Opens Doorway to Pacific"'.

114 Jane Perlez, 'Chinese Leader's Rise Came with New Attention to Dispute with Japan', *New York Times*, 2 December 2013.

115 Paul H.B. Godwin and Alice L. Miller, *China's Forbearance Has Limits: Chinese Threat and Retaliation Signaling and its Implications for Sino-American Military Confrontation*, China Strategic Perspectives no. 6 (Washington DC: Institute for National Strategic Studies, April 2013), p. 15.

116 Nicholas Szechenyi, Victor Cha, Bonnie S. Glaser, Michael J. Green and Christopher K. Johnson, 'China's Air Defense Identification Zone: Impact on Regional Security', Center for Strategic and International Studies, 26 November 2013, https://csis.org/publication/chinas-air-defense-identification-zone-impact-regional-security.

117 Jane Perlez, 'After Challenges, China Appears to Backpedal on Air Zone', *New York Times*, 27 November 2013.

118 Mark Beeson, 'Miscalculation or Test of Wills?', *Straits Times*, 3 December 2013.

119 Wen Yang, 'US "Trespass" Was Exactly What China Wanted', *Straits Times*, 2 December 2013.

120 Demetri Sevastopulo, 'China Air Zones Divides U.S. and Its Allies', *Financial Times*, 2 December 2013.

121 Hannah Beech, 'The U.S., Japan and South Korea Flout China's Air Defense Zone. What's a Superpower to Do?', *Time Online*, 29 November 2013.

122 Sevastopulo, 'China Air Zones Divides U.S. and Its Allies'.

123 Zhang Yiqian, 'Major US Airlines Heed Warning to Observe ADIZ Rules', *Global Times*, 2 December 2013.

124 William Choong, *Moving Towards Empathy: A Study of Three Sino-American Deterrence Episodes in the 20th Century*, PhD dissertation, Canberra: Australian National University, 2009, pp. 175–256.

# CHAPTER THREE

# Perceptions, postures and instability

China and Japan are, according to some observers, locked in a security dilemma, where mutual mistrust leads each to pursue defensive measures that the other regards as threatening.[1] Thomas Christensen argues that the memory of Japanese aggression in the 1930s and 1940s has helped create in China a fear about Japan's contemporary military. The increased military capabilities of Taiwan, for whom Japan is a potential ally, are also a factor.[2] Christensen maintains that there is little that Japan can do to change Chinese perceptions – the Chinese fear both the strengthening of the US–Japanese alliance (which would increase the scale of the military threat to China) as well as its breakdown (which would likely encourage Japan to build up its military without a restraining US influence).[3]

## Action–reaction dynamics

*Mutual perceptions*

In 1980, when China faced a potent and antagonistic Soviet Union, PLA Deputy Chief of Staff Wu Xiuquan said that he was 'all for Japan's increasing its self-defense capabilities … Generally speaking, Japan is one of the economic powers and it is entitled to becoming a big power militarily, too ... It would not seriously affect the Japanese economy even if defense spending were increased to 2 per cent of gross national product.'[4] As the Cold War wound down in the late 1980s, however, Chinese observers began to view Japan more warily. The historical perspective became more prevalent, stimulating a 'sincere and enduring' fear of Japanese militarism.[5] In 1987, Japan broke a 12-year, self-imposed limit of spending 1% of its GDP on defence. This was interpreted by China as Japan's arrival as a military power.

Japan's remilitarisation since the late 1980s has been constrained by pacifist inclinations, but this has not reduced Chinese fears of a growing militarism. Such perceptions were strengthened by Shinzo Abe's re-election in December 2012 and his rhetoric about Japan's return to the world stage and a strengthening of the JSDF to pre-empt future threats. One Chinese analyst underscored the wariness in Chinese circles about Abe's return and his bid for Japan to become a 'normal' country again: 'Japan is not a normal country. A country that reverts to militarism cannot be normal.'[6]

Chinese perceptions of the US–Japan alliance began to alter around this time as well. Previously, the US military had been viewed as a 'bottle cap' – that is, as a constraint on Japanese military power. Now the Chinese began to regard US forces as an 'eggshell', affording the Japanese military protective cover until such time as they were ready to act independently.[7] China saw itself as succeeding the Soviet Union as the focus of the US–Japan alliance. The alliance now sought to keep China out, but was no longer directed to keeping Japan down.[8] Joint research into theatre missile defence by the US and Japan beginning in the late 1990s was seen by the Chinese to be inherently threatening, as such defences could blunt China's relatively small nuclear arsenal.

China's view was largely informed by the policy of Washington and Tokyo towards Taiwan, which Beijing views as an integral part of one Chinese nation. In 1997 the guidelines for US–Japan security cooperation were revised, with Tokyo agreeing to provide logistical and other non-combat support to US military operations in 'areas surrounding Japan'.[9] This development sparked concerns in Beijing over the implications for China's claim to Taiwan. China's official media argued that the new guidelines were a 'dangerous' sign that that the US and Japan were 'stuck in a Cold War mode of thinking'. Evoking the spectre of Japan's 1937–45 invasion of China, the paper also maintained that the 'new guidelines ... will enable Japanese defense troops to go abroad "justifiably," something Japan has long dreamed of'.[10] In 2005, the US and Japan announced several new objectives, one of which was the 'peaceful resolution of issues concerning the Taiwan Strait'. Couched as it was together with other regional security objectives such as the maintenance of Japanese security, a peaceful unification of the Korean Peninsula and the welcoming of China's new role as a constructive power, the goal sounded innocuous enough.[11] But the Chinese saw it differently. A *People's Daily* report said that a genuine attempt by the US and Japan to bolster regional security should start with the upholding of the One China principle and doing nothing that would encourage separatist forces in Taiwan.[12]

By the 2000s, Chinese perceptions of a Japanese threat extended beyond Taiwan. A 2006 Chinese Defence White Paper noted that there were 'growing complexities' to China's security environment, including greater operational integration of US and Japanese forces, and Japan's plans to revise its constitution and shift to a more externally oriented military posture.[13] As Sino-Japanese tensions escalated over the Senkaku/Diaoyu Islands following the 2010 arrest of the Chinese trawler captain,

Beijing began to worry about Japan's increasingly strong line with regard to its territorial disputes with Russia, South Korea and China. Some Chinese observers described the tougher Japanese policy as 'hitting out in three directions', pointing out that Japan's intensification of its territorial disputes with several neighbours simultaneously was unprecedented in the post-war period. The train of logic was straightforward – if Japan pursued such assertive policies when it was militarily and constitutionally constrained, how aggressive might it be when those constraints were lifted and the country became 'normal' once again?[14] In China's 2013 Defence White Paper, Japan was criticised for 'making trouble over the issue of the Diaoyu Islands'.[15]

Japan's view of China began to change during the 1990s in parallel with changing Chinese perceptions of Japan. During the 1970s and 1980s, Japan was ambivalent about Chinese intentions and capabilities. Even as China's economy grew and its military began to modernise, Japan's long-standing feeling of superiority over China allayed potential fears. Moreover, in 2,000 years of history, there had only been a few instances of Chinese aggression toward Japan.[16] To some Japanese analysts, the strengthening of China was to be welcomed, as it was in line with their desire to be neither 'chaotic nor hegemonic'.[17]

This benign view changed as China's economic progress made it less of a supplicant for Japanese aid and investment, and more a regional rival. China's accelerating military modernisation, while fostering capabilities aimed at Taiwan, had disturbing implications for Japan and other countries in the region.[18] The lack of transparency around double-digit increases in Chinese defence spending created concern. In particular, what was revealed about Chinese capabilities and ambitions in missile technology and aerospace was unsettling to Japanese policymakers and analysts.[19] The 1995–96 Taiwan crisis demonstrated China's intent to use its military strength. Thus while North Korea remained the most immediate concern for Japanese decision-makers, China posed the greatest medium- to long-term challenge.[20] This perception was bolstered by China's augmentation of its ballistic- and cruise-missile capabilities, the upgrading of its air-defence and offence capabilities and its growing ambitions in space.[21]

Japanese perceptions reached a turning point in 2004, when China began regular naval and aerial forays in the vicinity of the Ryukyus, where the PLAN had shown no previous activity. In November, a Chinese *Han*-class nuclear-attack submarine conducted an intrusion into Japanese territorial waters when it passed through the strait between Ishigaki and Miyako islands at the southwestern end of the Sakishimas. In the previous month, the quasi-official Council on Security and Defense Capabilities issued a report analysing Japan's increasingly complex security environment, with a spectrum of threats ranging from terrorist attacks by non-state entities to 'very traditional warfare'. The so-called Araki report also highlighted security problems unique to Japan's location in East Asia, such as China's nuclear weapons and the possibility of armed clashes across the Taiwan Strait that could threaten Japan's security.[22] The 2004 National Defense Program Guidelines (NDPG), released one month after the PLAN's intrusion through the Ishigaki Strait, noted that China was modernising its nuclear and missile capabilities, as well as its naval and air forces, in order to expand its area of operations at sea, and that Japan would 'have to remain attentive to China's future actions'.[23]

The tone of subsequent Defense White Papers concerning China turned from quizzical to critical. The 2006 paper speculated on the motives behind China's military modernisation, dwelled on China's preparations for a potential war against

Taiwan and questioned whether 'the target of modernising troops exceeds the scope necessary for the national defence of China'.[24] More attention should be paid to the trend in 'stepped-up maritime activities by China, including operations of naval vessels and oceanographic research activities near Japan', the document said.[25] Two years later, the ongoing refurbishment of the Soviet-era *Varyag* aircraft carrier by the PLAN stimulated much debate as to whether China's naval strategy should extend from offshore waters ('green water') to the high seas ('blue water'). A paper by the National Institute of Defense Studies (NIDS) in Japan noted that a good definition of 'blue water' had been offered by Chinese Admiral Liu Huaqing, who in the 1980s formulated a push for the PLAN's theatre of operation from the First Island Chain (which includes Taiwan and the Ryukyu Islands) to the northern Pacific Ocean and the Second Island Chain (which extends from Japan to Guam) (see Map 2), in conjunction with China's economic growth, rising standards of science and technology and further strengthening of the navy. NIDS' *East Asia Security Review 2008* summarised China's progress in this regard:

> Taken together, the aircraft carrier development program, the emergence of a doctrinal framework for high-seas operation, the enhancement of blue-water supply capabilities, and the normalization of blue-water activity should be interpreted as signs that China has already started to establish a presence on the high seas. This trend should be closely monitored, not only because it represents a potential threat to China's neighbors and a possible source of friction with such powers as the United States and India, but also because it will have an impact on sea lanes that are a lifeline for Japan.[26]

The 2010 NDPG, released after a marked escalation in Sino-Japanese tensions over the Senkakus/Diaoyus, used uncharacteristically strong language. It noted the rapid modernisation of China's nuclear and missile forces, as well as its navy and air force, and highlighted that China had been 'intensifying its maritime activities in the surrounding waters'. These trends, coupled with 'insufficient transparency' over China's military forces and security policy, constituted a 'concern for the regional and global community'. The 2010 NDPG marked a shift from the Cold War-era Basic Defense Force concept, based on the deployment of heavy weapons and infantry on the Home Islands to deter an invasion, to a Dynamic Defense Force concept, with highly flexible and mobile units used to address complex contingencies, such as an invasion of Japan's outlying islands.[27] The 2010 guidelines also highlighted the growing number of 'gray zone' disputes over territory, sovereignty and economic interests.[28] Not surprisingly, China slammed the report as 'irresponsible', saying that it reflected a misunderstanding of Chinese intentions.[29]

The tone of Japan's 2013 Defense White Paper was even more strident. This was not unexpected, given that it was published six months after the 'radar lock' incident near the disputed islands. The paper noted that China had engaged in 'dangerous acts' around Japan's waters and airspace, giving rise to 'contingency situations' such as the 'radar lock' incident.[30] The 2013 document removed phrasing from the 2012 Defense White Paper about 'welcoming' China's emergence as a world power and its role concurrent with that status. Instead, the 2013 Defense White Paper said that Japan 'strongly expected' China to recognise its responsibility as a major power and stick to international norms. It added that in its territorial disputes with surrounding countries, including Japan, China had been attempting to 'change the status quo by force' based on assertions which were 'incompatible with international law'.[31] The same themes were espoused by Abe at the 2014 Shangri-La Dialogue in Singapore, where he stressed that territorial claims had to be 'based on international law' and eschew the use of 'force or coercion'.[32]

## Military postures in the Senkakus/Diaoyus

China's growing interests in the Ryukyu Islands were underlined in the country's 2010 Defence White Paper, which discussed China's 'vast territories and territorial seas' and pledged to 'defend the security of China's lands, inland waters, territorial waters and airspace' and 'safeguard maritime rights and interests'.[33] The document outlined an 'offshore defence strategy', but did not specify the missions and capabilities involved. American sources, both official and scholarly, detail the main characteristics of the Chinese 'offshore defence' concept (also translated as 'near-seas defence').[34] Proposed first by Deng Xiaoping in 1979, the strategy was subsequently fleshed out by Admiral Liu Huaqing. Near-seas defence is a successor to the PLAN's previous coastal-defence mission, which called on the PLAN to defend China's coasts from the Soviet Pacific Fleet in what was predicted to be a largely land-based war.[35] The near-seas defence strategy was assigned to the PLAN around 1985, making it an independent service with an independent mission for the first time.[36]

According to Admiral Liu, near-seas active defence is defined as covering (1) the First Island Chain, which stretches from the Kurile Islands through the islands of Japan, the Ryukyus, Taiwan, the Philippines and Borneo; (2) the Yellow Sea, East China Sea and South China Sea, or the three near seas within the inner rims of the First Island Chain, and (3) sea areas adjacent to the outer rims of this island chain, including those of the North Pacific.[37] Near-seas active defence has several aims: the reunification of Taiwan, restoration of lost and disputed maritime territories, protection of China's maritime resources and the security of major sea lanes of communication in times of war, deterrence and defence against foreign aggression from sea, and strategic nuclear deterrence.[38] Advocates of offshore defence argued that it was necessary to extend the maritime active defence perimeter in order to protect China's vulnerable maritime flank and reduce the efficacy of adversaries' long-range precision-strike capabilities.[39]

Nan Li, a scholar at the US Naval War College, has outlined five war-fighting objectives that could derive from the PLAN's near-seas strategy:

> 'Blockade and isolation' … involves the employment of water mines, submarines and air capabilities to establish a layered blockade of the opponent's naval bases and harbors, sea lanes and water areas. The purpose is to prevent the opponent's ships from exiting bases and harbors in order to enhance the strike effect. The other is 'joint strike', which refers to the use of conventional missile, air, naval and special operations capabilities to strike the opponent's reconnaissance and early warning systems, command and control, naval and air bases and logistics infrastructure, for the purpose of crippling the opponent's capabilities to counter the PLAN's sea-control operations. The third method is 'suppression of outlaying islands', which involves the use of coastal firepower, ground-attack aircraft and light surface combatants to strike the defense systems of these islands. This serves the purpose of suppressing and reducing their role as the forward platforms for countering sea-control and amphibious-landing operations. The fourth method is 'search and annihi-

lation', which involves the use of submarines, major surface combatants and sea-attack aircraft to search and destroy the opponent's major naval combatants outside the blocked areas, for the purpose of capturing and maintaining sea-control. Such a method may involve flanking movements, deception, and inducement and compulsion to lure the opponent's ships into the designated sea areas, thus creating favorable fighting opportunities. The final method is 'comprehensive barrier removal', which refers to employing various means to remove the threat of water mines to ensure the security and freedom of sea-crossing and amphibious landing operations.[40]

Of these five mission objectives, three – 'joint strike', 'search and annihilation' and 'comprehensive barrier removal' – could have direct applications to a Senkaku/Diaoyu contingency. Japan's radar and signals-intelligence facilities on islands such as Miyako could be 'primary targets' under the PLAN's 'joint strike' objective, as are ISR systems or mobile forces deployed to the Sakishimas in the future.[41] 'Search and annihilation' and 'comprehensive barrier' objectives would also deny mobile forces the ability to conduct sea-control missions. If China aimed to seize the Senkakus/Diaoyus or other islands in the Sakishima chain during a Taiwan crisis, it would be, as Sayers puts it, 'forced to vie for sea control with Japanese and U.S. forces'.[42] Given that the near-seas active defence strategy covers the Japanese-controlled Ryukyus (which include the Senkakus/ Diaoyus) and Taiwan, it bears repeating that the Ryukyus and Taiwan are intimately linked in terms of strategic significance. Yonaguni Island, at the southwestern tip of the Ryukyus, is only 110km from Taiwan. During the 1996 Taiwan Strait crisis, when the PLA targeted missiles into Taiwanese waters off the island's two main ports in a bid to influence the presidential election, one of the 'test' missiles reportedly landed within 60km of Yonaguni.[43]

China's near-seas strategy is also supported by hardware acquisitions that will bear directly on any future Senkaku/ Diaoyu contingency (see Table 3). Since the early 1990s, China has prioritised naval procurement, as a doctrinal shift has occurred from the personnel-intensive and land-focused principles of Maoist 'People's War' towards the capability to wage regional, high-tech wars. This has included commissioning high-tech, capable and indigenously built naval vessels. The Type 052D destroyer, the first of which was commissioned in March 2014, boasts stealth technology, a new active phased-array radar, improved and larger naval gunnery and, perhaps most significantly, a 64-cell vertical launching system that could field a newly developed land-attack cruise missile in the future. The Type 052D sits alongside the *Jiangkai* II-class (Type 054A) frigate, first commissioned in 2007, and the *Jiangdao*-class (Type 056) corvette, first commissioned in 2012. These modern vessels are being produced in large numbers: eight Type 052D vessels, 20 Type 054A frigates and 22 Type 056 corvettes were in the water or under construction as of late 2014.[44] Other vessel classes produced in China since the mid-1990s have largely comprised just one or two ships of each class. This indicates that the PLAN is now satisfied that its 'leapfrog' strategy of learning about ship design and handling has been successful, and it can now develop a sizeable fleet with tiers of combatants to defend littoral waters and project modest power beyond China's shores.

Together, the new destroyers and frigates represent a significant upgrade to the PLAN's area air-defence capability.[45] In China's East Sea Fleet, which would be directly involved in any Senkaku/Diaoyu contingency, the 3rd Destroyer Flotilla received two *Jiangkai* I-class (Type 054) frigates in 2005–06 and two *Jiangkai* II-class frigates in 2008. By the end of 2014, its sister 6th Destroyer Flotilla will be the most advanced surface warfare formation in the PLAN, having received four *Luyang* II-class (Type 052C) destroyers in 2013–14 and four *Jiangkai* II-class frigates in 2011–14.[46]

Two new squadrons of *Houbei*-class (Type 022) fast-attack craft based at Shipuzhen and Fuding could have a role in any East China Sea contingency.[47] Introduced in 2004, the *Houbei* class is a new type of anti-ship cruise missile (ASCM)-armed fast-attack craft that uses a stealthy, wave-piercing catamaran hull. Each vessel can carry 8 C-802 ASCMs with a range of about 50nm.[48] Since the small in-water profile and high speed (estimated to be at least 36 knots) of the *Houbei* class would make it difficult to hit with torpedoes or ASCMs, the fast-attack craft could be used against carrier strike groups. This would allow a modern, cruise-missile-focused realisation of swarming tactics – a traditional PLAN concept.[49] In a Senkaku/Diaoyu scenario, *Houbei*-class catamarans could hold off enemy forces while the PLAN fleet pounded away at shore targets.[50] This was demonstrated in PLAN live-fire exercises conducted in a relatively small area off Zhejiang Province between 30 June and 5 July 2010. The core theme of the naval combined-arms operations involved ASCM launches by surface ships, and included *Houbei*-class vessels.[51] As part of an anti-access/area-denial (A2/AD) strategy that seeks to deter third-party intervention, particularly by the US, the PLA has also deployed systems that can engage enemy surface ships up to 1,000nm from China's coast (for comparison, the Senkaku/Diaoyu Islands lie about 180nm offshore). China is fielding an array of conventionally armed ballistic missiles, ground- and air-launched land-attack cruise missiles, special-operations forces and cyber-warfare capabilities to hold targets at risk throughout the region.[52] According to Japan's 2013 Defense White Paper, China has a large number of solid-propellant DF-15 and DF-11 short-range ballistic missiles (SRBMs). While they are 'believed to be deployed against Taiwan', the SRBMs also cover a part of the Southwestern Islands, including the Senkakus (which, the document stressed, were 'inherent territories of Japan').[53]

Tokyo's growing wariness about China's military development, the dispute over the Senkaku/Diaoyus, and what has been described as a security 'vacuum' in the outlying islands have driven Japan's new focus on the Southwestern Islands (see Table 4). Speaking to reporters at the release of the 2010 NDPG in December of that year, Japanese Defense Minister Toshimi Kitazawa described the southwest region as a 'vacant' area that was addressed strategically in the 2010 NDPG, with specific steps to be taken according to the Mid-Term Defense Programme for Fiscal Years 2011–15.[54] This included the establishment by the JSDF of a new first-response unit in the Southwestern Islands to gather intelligence, monitor situations and 'respond swiftly when incidents occur'.[55] Press reports indicated that the Defense Ministry had intended to deploy 100 non-combatant Japan Ground Self Defense Force personnel to Yonaguni Island and had considered deploying personnel to Miyako and Ishigaki islands as well.[56] The JASDF would also shift one fighter squadron to Naha Air Base, so that there would be two fighter squadrons there to provide 'rapid response' capability to the Southwestern Islands. Transport helicopters (CH-47JA) would continue to be acquired to improve effective response capabilities and to ensure rapid deployment to the Southwestern Islands. Simultaneously, a successor to the current transport aircraft (C-1) would be introduced. To ensure the security of sea lanes in areas including southwestern Japan, new helicopter destroyers, destroyers and fixed-wing patrol aircraft (P-1) would be acquired.[57]

Japan's 2013 Defense Posture Review proposed strengthening ISR capabilities (for example by introducing high-altitude, long-endurance unmanned aerial vehicles) and stressed that air superiority and command of the sea must be maintained to be able to respond effectively to attacks on Japan's remote islets [58] – a veiled reference to potential scenarios involving the Chinese military. The document stressed that mobile- and amphibious-deployment capabilities would be important to get troops rapidly to such areas in contingencies.[59]

Amphibious forces would enhance Japan's ability to contend with China's active maritime presence, in particular to defend the Senkaku/Diaoyu Islands. The core of the Dynamic Defense Force concept introduced in 2010 is operational readiness for crisis response. In the case of amphibious forces, this is a joint pursuit integrating the efforts of all three services.[60] The Dynamic Defense Force concept builds on actions taken in recent years by Japanese decision-makers to move 'from an SDF that simply exists to an SDF that actually works', as then-Defense Minister Shigeru Ishiba put it in a 2004 Defense White Paper.[61] In 2012, an appreciation of Chinese sensitivities led Japan and the US to cancel manoeuvres involving the retaking from an enemy force of a small island south of Okinawa, planned for their 18-day biennial *Operation Keen Sword* in November, involving 34,000 Japanese and 10,000 American soldiers, six vessels and 360 aircraft. Although the island of Irisunajima lies hundreds of kilometres from the disputed Senkakus/Diaoyus, an invasion exercise was considered too provocative, given that the CCP was scheduled to hold its 18th Party Congress in October.[62]

In June 2013, however, a contingent of 1,000 JSDF personnel from all three services took part in *Operation Dawn Blitz*, a two-week training exercise with US marines that involved a large-scale amphibious assault. In their most ambitious amphibious exercise to that point, a few hundred JSDF personnel with helicopters embarked on three JMSDF ships, gaining familiarity with the vessels during the transit from Japan.[63] They practised complex ship-to-shore operations to enhance the allies' ability to defend Japan's outlying islands, and carried out the first-ever landing of a US Marine Corps *Osprey* aircraft on the deck of the JMSDF helicopter carrier *Hyuga*.[64] The sharp end of the spear for the JSDF would be the 700-strong Western Army Infantry Regiment, which top Japanese officers admit will take some time to duplicate the suite of capabilities held by the US marines.[65] *Operation Dawn Blitz* was clearly orchestrated with an eye on China and its growing military capabilities. One analyst said that a strengthening of the US-Japan alliance was required lest it 'buckle' to China.[66]

Japan's military build-up in the Southwestern Islands has attracted considerable attention from China. In November 2013, as part of *Operation Keen Sword*, Japan announced that it was temporarily deploying Type-88 surface-to-ship missiles on Miyako Island, the first time that missile systems had been deployed there.[67] Coincidentally, the exercise took place around the same time that the US-based RAND Corporation released a research report proposing that Japan turn China's A2/AD strategy on its head by adopting a 'far blockade' strategy using land-based anti-ship missiles (ASMs) at chokepoints in the Pacific. Such missiles would constitute 'inexpensive joint force multipliers' that would raise the costs of a conflict for China; and should deterrence fail, such a strategy would limit China's ability to inflict damage off the Asian mainland.[68] The RAND report adds to a growing list of literature on the strategic options that Japan could employ in the Southwestern Islands. Other suggested options include offensive mine-laying, fortification of the islands against attack, the obstruction of chokepoints with submarines, the consistent presence of JSDF and US armed forces in the region to bolster dynamic deterrence, 'tripwire' deterrence, a 'mosquito fleet' strategy and comprehensive area denial.[69]

China's growing confidence that the balance of comprehensive national power will shift in its favour at the expense of Japan, and a concurrent Japanese realisation of this attitude, have added to Tokyo's sense of 'resentment and insecurity'.[70] In the view of three China watchers, the two countries are engaged in a potentially 'destructive action–reaction cycle fuelled by deep populist antipathy and historical resentment toward one another'.[71] This is evident in the exchange of rhetoric between China and Japan in 2013 about their respective military postures, as well as in two large-scale military exercises conducted by China and Japan late that year.

In July 2013, a Chinese Defence Ministry spokesman said that China was 'discontented and resolutely against' allegations made in Japan's 2013 Defense White Paper, concerning repeated Chinese intrusions in Japanese territorial waters and airspace and China's use of aggressive tactics to expand its maritime power. The spokesman added that it was Japan, not China, that was undermining regional stability with its claims to the disputed Diaoyu Islands. This was seen to be an unusually strong rebuttal from China, which rarely singles out other countries by name.

In August, China called on Japan to abide by its policy of peaceful development and warned against Japan's military expansion, after Tokyo unveiled the *Izumo*, a 27,000-tonne helicopter carrier. Japan's neighbours and the global community should be 'highly vigilant' about Japan's military expansion, the Chinese Defence Ministry said.[72] The *Izumo* can carry out missions such as anti-submarine warfare (ASW) as well as humanitarian assistance and disaster relief (HADR) missions. Chinese analysts regard the *Izumo*'s ASW capabilities – when operating in tandem with the US Navy's new *Aegis* destroyers and ISR capabilities – as, in one observer's words, 'quietly building the ability to counter China's A2/AD strategy'.[73]

In October 2013, China conducted a pioneering naval drill in the Western Pacific. The *Maneuver-5* exercise involved the deployment of ten naval vessels from three PLAN fleets – the Northern, Eastern and Southern Fleets – which crossed the First Island Chain and gathered in the maritime area between the first and second chains. The ships – four guided-missile destroyers, five guided-missile frigates and one replenishment oiler – were supported by two H-6 strategic bombers and two Y-8 airborne early-warning and control aircraft. A researcher at the PLA Academy of Military Science said that the so-called 'First Island Chain' had been 'dismembered' by the three major fleets and that the island chains blockade of the PLAN was no longer operative.[74] The exercise set the stage for Beijing's imposition of an ADIZ the following month, and fed China's growing narrative about its ability to break through what it saw to be an American attempt to 'encircle' or 'contain' China and prevent the PLAN from operating freely in the Western Pacific.[75] The following month, Japan and the US conducted *Operation Keen Sword*, which included the placement of surface-to-ship missiles on Miyako Island.[76] The timing of the exercise was a clear signal that Japan was willing to defend the disputed Senkaku/Diaoyu Islands.

In November 2013, it was Japan's turn to argue that China was undermining the status quo in the region. On 23 November, China declared its ADIZ covering part of the East China Sea and the Senkakus/Diaoyus. China maintained the ADIZ was a 'justified act of self-defence' and not aimed at any specific country.[77] At a press conference on 29 November, Foreign

Minister Fumio Kishida said that China's establishment of the ADIZ 'unilaterally changes the status quo, escalates the situation and could cause unintended consequences'.[78] At an ASEAN–Japan summit in Tokyo in December, Abe argued that the ADIZ constituted an attempt by China to violate the freedom of aviation over the high seas, a general principle of international law. Abe called for China to 'rescind all measures like this that unjustly violate the general rule'.[79] In response, a Chinese Foreign Ministry spokesman said that China took offense that Abe had used 'an international occasion to maliciously slander China'.[80]

## The erosion of stability

During the second half of the twentieth century, four factors supported stability in the Senkaku/Diaoyu Islands. Firstly, nationalist sentiments in both China and Japan were restrained by their domestic political arrangements and the exigencies of the Cold War. Secondly, there was the implicit agreement to shelve the dispute from 1972 onwards.

Thirdly, where disputes arose, diplomats in both states practised 'ritualised management' to ensure that tensions did not spiral out of control. Ming Wan noted that the dialectical nature of such ritualised management led to greater tensions that nonetheless remained within acceptable boundaries:

> Previous dispute management has an impact on subsequent disputes, providing a script and parameters for pushing and pulling. On the other hand, repeated interaction ameliorates disputes by playing them out and allowing both sides to vent. And repeated interaction allows the two countries to quarrel over things within safe limits because they know each other and know the boundaries.[81]

Fourthly, the military balance between the two powers was favourable to Japan and thus supported the status quo of Japanese control over the islands. Tokyo possessed the region's most capable navy and it still holds an edge over its Chinese counterpart.[82] In addition, Japan's military was backed by US security guarantees that extend to the disputed islands.

Since the beginning of the twenty-first century, these factors have all declined or disappeared, and the scope for conflict is now significantly wider. Restraints on nationalist sentiment and policies have weakened in both states. In 1990s China, nationalism emerged as a potent force. Often it mirrored the CCP line, but it was independent of the party's hegemony.[83] The rapid penetration of the Internet and social media eroded the party's control over popular sentiment and began to influence policymaking. Following the government's September 2012 announcement of baselines for the territorial waters of the Diaoyus, expectations were raised that China would take steps to reassert sovereignty over the islands. After CMS vessels arrived near the islands, however, Internet users questioned the government's resolve and mocked the CMS for cowardice.[84] Some netizens even called for military intervention, while others called the Foreign Ministry 'mai guo bu' (Ministry of Traitors) for asking Japan to return to talks. The Chinese leadership, in inculcating anti-Japanese sentiment through the country's education system, contributed to this surge of anti-Japanese nationalism. Beijing is left with a dilemma – either 'ride the anti-Japanese tiger' that their propaganda has created, or back down and risk a domestic backlash.[85]

Since the turn of the century Japan also saw an upsurge in nationalism, in part due to China's growing assertiveness in the global arena and the establishment of a *Bao Diao* (Protect Diaoyu) movement.[86]. In March 2004, the Japanese Diet passed a resolution on the Senkakus for the first time, calling for the

preservation of territorial integrity and asking the government to take 'all possible and precautionary steps' towards
that end.[87] The following year, Yukio Edano, chief of the
Constitution Research Committee of the DPJ, then in opposition, proposed that JSDF troops be stationed in the Senkakus
to prevent incursions by other countries.[88] The suggestion was
mirrored by Abe in December 2012. During the heat of the election campaign, Abe said that civil servants should be stationed
on the islands. In August 2013, Hayao Miyazaki, a popular
director of animated children's films, was lauded for produc-
ing 'The Wind Rises', a tribute to the 'extraordinary genius' of
the Imperial Japanese Army's *Zero* fighter aircraft. But he was
on the receiving end of an outpouring of hatred after he challenged the revision of Japan's pacifist constitution and chided
Abe for airbrushing history.[89]

Since the late 1980s, too, there has been a slow and gradual
unravelling of the implicit agreement to put aside or shelve the
territorial dispute. In 1992, China introduced a new maritime
law that effectively claimed the islands as sovereign Chinese
territory. Nihon Seinensha (Japanese Youth Federation)
sparked several incidents over the islands, by erecting a lighthouse on Uotsuri/Diaoyu Dao in September 1978, enlarging it
in 1988 and building another on Kitakojima in 1996.[90] Japan's
'nationalisation' of the islands in 2012 to pre-empt their
purchase by a right-wing politician later triggered a furious
response in China.

Diplomats in both countries who believe it is vital to make the
bilateral relationship work have lost influence.[91] The Japanese
Foreign Ministry was weakened by scandals in 2001 and its
'China School' has encountered internal opposition. A similar
process has served to weaken the 'Japan School' in the Chinese
Foreign Ministry.[92] More importantly, the generation of politicians who were instrumental in the normalisation of relations

in the 1970s has passed on. For example, Liao Chengzhi – the dean of China's Japan policy team who worked under Zhou Enlai – died in 1983. On the Japanese side, Hiromu Nonaka was considered the last old-style 'pipe' with China.[93]

From 2013 onwards, both countries' leading politicians were nationalists with little interest in forging a working relationship with one another. After Xi took power as the leader of the CCP in November 2012, he gave few signs that he was ready to expend political capital on de-escalating tensions in the East China Sea. One of his early speeches urged the PLA to be combat-ready.[94] Japanese analysts largely agree that, in China, the goodwill towards Japan that accumulated during the years of Hu Jintao and Wen Jiabao all but dissipated with the ascent of Xi Jinping. Yang Jiechi, who had good American connections and was close to Xi, initiated a hardening of China's policy towards Japan[95] and favoured isolating Tokyo. Moreover, given rising anti-Japanese sentiment in China it has become untenable for Chinese politicians to take an accommodating position towards Tokyo.[96] One Japanese analyst put it more pointedly: there has been a near-complete breakdown of the ritualised management system. The pro-China Tanaka faction in the LDP was decimated by Koizumi during his tenure as prime minister. Secondly, the link between Komeito (the LDP's junior partner in government) and China has weakened. Finally, the number of diplomats on either side who support stronger bilateral relations has decreased.[97] Another analyst, a former Japanese diplomat, said that he once put great store in the relationship. Given current tensions and difficulties, however, the only viable choice for Japan was to implement a strategy of 'dialogue and deterrence' vis-à-vis China.[98] Chinese analysts feel likewise – it would be hard to return to the 1972 agreement, given the nationalism of the Abe government.

It has thus been difficult for diplomats and politicians to forge even a modicum of cooperation in the relationship. After the 2010 arrest of the Chinese boat captain, the sides agreed to negotiate a separate communications mechanism that involved several layers, including law-enforcement agencies, militaries and foreign ministries. A first round of talks was held in May 2012, but a second round was scuttled after the September 2012 nationalisation of the Senkakus.[99] A clandestine summit between a senior Chinese Foreign Ministry official and his Japanese counterpart was held in Tokyo in early October 2013, but the talks appeared to have gained little traction.[100]

The most obvious factor that has contributed to a loss of stability is China's decision to challenge and thereby erode Japan's control over the islands, bit by bit. This reflects a widely held belief in China that Japan could cement its de facto control of the islands if its control regime runs unchallenged for 50 years, based on the legal doctrine of 'acquisition prescription'.[101] By their incursions into the waters surrounding the islands, the Chinese are seeking to change the status quo and they have become more assertive over time, from the activist landing in 2004 to the insertion of research ships in 2007 and shipping vessels thereafter, significantly increasing from 2012 on; the commencement of intrusions into the islands' airspace; lodging of its maritime claims with the UN; the 'radar lock' incident and the imposition of the ADIZ.

## Potential stabilisers

### The US role

If the Japan–China relationship lacks the factors necessary to stabilise the conflict over the islands, the US and the emerging regional security architecture might take up the slack. The US is the leading power in the region and has made clear repeatedly that it 'does not take a position on the question of the ultimate sovereignty of the Senkaku Islands'.[102] The US sees itself as impartial with regard to the dispute. After Beijing implemented its ADIZ over the East China Sea in November 2013, US Vice President Joe Biden did not join in Japan's call for the zone to be scrapped; rather, he called on both sides to take steps to lower tensions.[103] He underscored the need for crisis-management mechanisms and 'effective channels of communications' between China and Japan to reduce the risk of escalation.

To China, however, such nuances do not make the US an impartial player: it is anything but, given its security guarantee to Japan over the islands. Responding to Biden's call for crisis-management measures for the East China Sea, an editorial in the *China Daily* said that, despite Washington's claim to be an impartial mediator, the US had 'obviously taken Japan's side'.[104] US national interests also figure in the dispute. Since 1972 the US military has leased from Japan two islets in the Senkakus group – Kuba and Taisho – as a bombing range.[105]

The US security guarantee over Japan – and by extension, the Senkakus/Diaoyus – serves to reassure Tokyo and to deter Beijing. Throughout the 1970s and 1980s, the US signalled to Japan in careful language that the Mutual Security Treaty would apply to the islands. A briefing paper prepared for US National Security Advisor Kissinger in 1972 stated that the alliance 'could be interpreted' to apply to the islands.[106] In recent years, US reassurances on this point have become more consistent and robust. In October 2010, Hillary Clinton, US secretary of state, affirmed the islands fell within the scope of Article 5 of the US–Japan Treaty of Mutual Cooperation and Security.[107] However, in February 2013, Abe apparently failed to get ironclad assurances from Barack Obama over Washington's commitment to defend the Senkakus.[108] This was seized upon by analysts who perceive an element of ambiguity within the

US guarantee to Japan; they complain that the 'weasel words' of the US have not contributed to stability, but have only rattled America's allies.[109]

US efforts to deter China and reassure Japan could fail in one of two ways. Firstly, the security guarantee could embolden Japan to act recklessly. To address this risk, Mira Rapp-Hopper suggests that the US guarantee might vary according to circumstances: if China were to escalate tensions, the US security guarantee could be reasonably invoked; but if the Japanese were guilty of provocation, such as the 2012 purchase of the islands, the guarantee would not be assured.[110] This is the view of Chinese analysts, who argue that the US could be dragged into a Sino-Japanese conflict if Washington is not careful.[111] Indeed, the drawing of a 'red line' in the Senkaku/Diaoyu Islands might be counterproductive, given that it would raise the risk of miscalculation and runs counter to the careful and creative diplomacy that would ultimately be required to bring China and Japan back from the brink.

Secondly, China might not view the US security guarantee over the disputed islands as credible. During the Taiwan Strait crisis in 1995–96, a Chinese general reportedly told US Assistant Secretary of Defense Charles Freeman that American leaders would 'care more about Los Angeles than they do about Taiwan'. China, the general said, would act militarily against Taiwan without fear of US intervention.[112] There are inherent problems with extended deterrence, when the focus of deterrent efforts is also a nuclear power. During the Cold War, US allies and adversaries alike pondered whether the US would be willing to risk the destruction of New York or Washington in the defence of Tokyo and Berlin. At least during the Cold War, credibility was enhanced by the global, ideological nature of the US–Soviet struggle. The competition between the US and China in the early twenty-first century is not comparable, for it is neither global nor ideological, and there is considerable scope for cooperation and perhaps ultimately a partnership. Although the US has security commitments to Japan, it is pursuing strategic dialogue with China at the highest levels. In September 2012, US Secretary of Defense Leon Panetta announced the stationing of a new missile-defence radar in Japan; but on the next day, he arrived in China with a view to building better military-to-military ties with Beijing. Similarly, Chuck Hagel, Panetta's successor, repeated a similar declaration of the US security guarantee over the Senkaku Islands in April 2014; but days later, he was given a tour of China's first aircraft carrier, the *Liaoning* (formerly the *Varyag*) as Beijing sought to improve the military-to-military relationship between China and America. These broader concerns may have a significant effect on how the US deals with Japan in times of difficulty.[113]

The US could lower the risks of conflict over the Senkaku/Diaoyu Islands by tempering its security guarantee with more ambiguity, thereby lowering the risks of escalation and brinkmanship. This would be akin to the ambiguity that the US practised during the Taiwan Strait crisis of 1995–96. At that time, US officials refused requests by their Chinese counterparts to discuss contingency plans, saying only that they stood for peaceful resolution of the issue and that Chinese use of force against Taiwan would be a serious mistake. When pressed further, Assistant Secretary of Defense Joseph Nye couched his reply in the spirit of the Taiwan Relations Act: he told Chinese leaders that 'we don't know and you don't know' exactly how the US would respond to Chinese action against Taiwan.[114] Theoretically, at least, a less explicit security assurance would give the US a degree of flexibility and give China and Japan an incentive to behave with circumspection, while preserving deterrence at a lower risk of escalation.[115]

The prospects of the US adopting a nuanced approach are low, however. The US has typically hewn to a classic deterrent posture with regard to the Senkakus, similar to the fashion in which Hagel stressed American defence commitments to Japan during a visit to Beijing in April 2014. At a press briefing, General Chang Wanquan, Hagel's Chinese counterpart, stressed that China had 'indisputable sovereignty' over the Diaoyu Islands, and for effect, stressed that the Chinese military could 'assemble as soon as summoned, fight any battle and win'. Hagel countered Chang's remarks by saying that Japan and the Philippines were 'long-time allies of the United States'. He added that the US was 'fully committed' to its treaty obligations to the two countries.[116] To adopt a more ambiguous position would also be counterproductive because in Japan there is a growing constituency that doubts US commitment to the security guarantee. Tokyo was infuriated when Biden said that Washington's ties with Beijing constituted a 'new model of great power relations'. In Japan's view, this sanctioned a new regional regime led by China.[117]

The possibility of the US acceding to China a greater regional role has been mooted by Zbigniew Brzezinski, who served as US national security advisor in the Carter administration. Brzezinski has argued that the US and China could form a G2 to tackle financial crises, climate change and the proliferation of nuclear weapons.[118] The two powers have sought to work on their core interests in a bid to reduce the competitive and even conflictual elements of their relationship. Andrew Nathan, for example, argues that China is advancing its core interests to articulate what it regards as a reasonable basis on which it can expect the US to accommodate China in Asia. If both sides were to agree on which interests were truly 'core' to each, then both powers could agree to a new division of influence.[119] For China, the main focus would be on the East and South China seas, to create an extensive security buffer off the Chinese coast and give Beijing control of valuable offshore fisheries and seabed energy and mineral resources.[120]

Such a power-sharing arrangement is not unprecedented. In three major episodes of Sino-American interaction in the second half of the twentieth century – the Korean War in 1950–53, the war in Vietnam in the 1960s and the 1995–96 Taiwan Strait crisis – both China and the US showed an ability to understand and appreciate the strategic goals of the other, leading to outcomes which lowered tensions and led to confidence building.[121] In March 2013 US National Security Advisor Tom Donilon challenged the concept of the 'Thucydides Trap' – that a rising power and an established power were destined for conflict.[122] He called on the US and China to 'build a new model of relations between an existing power and an emerging one'.[123]

If the US and China were able to create a G2, based on each respecting the other's core interests, it would probably involve an understanding on the Senkaku/Diaoyu Islands. This could take the form of the US forswearing any intervention in a Sino-Japanese conflict over the islands, in return for Chinese commitments to work on a legally binding code of conduct for the South China Sea dispute, or increased efforts to get North Korea to reduce or even eradicate its nuclear arsenal. A US–China grand bargain, however, would be difficult to negotiate, both between the parties and within each country's political system. Moreover, while certainly favourable for China's claim on the islands, it would not promise stability or peace in the East China Sea. Japan might respond by adopting a more autonomous foreign and defence policy, and even acquire its own nuclear arsenal. Japan is not alone in its assessment that America's broad support for China's proposal for a 'new type of great power relations' is just another euphemism for a Group of 2. Other Asian countries share the Japanese view.[124]

## Regional security architecture

Asia's security architecture has developed markedly in the past 25 years, although this has had little real impact on the region's strategic challenges, such as major shifts in the balance of power, skewed distributions of economic weight, political and cultural heterogeneity, territorial disputes and anaemic security institutionalism.[125] According to one estimate, there are over 100 security dialogue channels in the region at Track-1 level and more than 200 at the unofficial Track-2 level.[126] Among these channels, some regional institutions stand out – the ASEAN Regional Forum (ARF), the Asia-Pacific Economic Cooperation Leaders' Meeting (APEC), the East Asia Summit (EAS), ASEAN Defence Ministers' Meeting Plus (ADMM-Plus), the Shangri-La Dialogue and the Six-Party Talks for the denuclearisation of North Korea.

In theory at least, this should be positive for the Sino-Japanese relationship. An 'open and inclusive' regional architecture would dampen fears that the region could be dominated by either a US–Chinese condominium or a concert of powers. Regional bodies such as the EAS and ADMM-Plus reflect the values and principles of ASEAN, a grouping of small states, with normative values such as respect of territorial integrity and sovereignty, the peaceful settlement of disputes, non-interference in the internal affairs of nations, consensus-based decisions and equality of states.[127] As Amitav Acharya notes, Asian security institutions have done well in the spread of cooperative security norms (such as ASEAN's Treaty of Amity and Cooperation), the engagement of former adversaries (ASEAN and Vietnam, China and the former Soviet Union, India and Pakistan), the involvement of all major powers of the world (China, the European Union, India, Russia and the US) and the 'simultaneous engagement' of the US and China.[128] The extension of these institutions could help to resolve the disputes that imperil Sino-Japanese relations. Increased cooperation between China and Japan would be assisted and stabilised by the exogenous development of a regional security community.

One should, however, not be too enamoured by the pace and development of such regional structures. It is largely a work in progress and has yet to contribute to regional stability, let alone Sino-Japanese relations, in a significant way. As Graeme Dobell notes, the emerging Asian system of regional institutions – which involves the bolting together of an emerging (but not emerged) G2, a nascent Asian concert of major powers and the existing base of US alliances – is a 'total conceptual mess'.[129] More importantly, there is also a sequencing problem between the development of regional security institutions and the trajectory of Sino-Japanese relations. Sino-Japanese reconciliation is more likely a precondition for the flourishing of regional institutions, rather than an outcome of that development. As Zhang Tuosheng notes:

> Continued development of China–Japan relations will inject vigour into, and lay down the foundation for, the development of multilateral security mechanisms in East Asia. History will prove that only once China and Japan achieve genuine reconciliation, and are able to cooperate comprehensively, can East Asia establish an effective multilateral security cooperation mechanism.[130]

Even if reconciliation between China and Japan were to progress substantively, it would take some time, perhaps decades, for growing Sino-Japanese comity and regional security mechanisms to mutually reinforce. For instance, ARF has yet to move from preventive diplomacy to conflict resolution. In the South China Sea dispute between China and several ASEAN countries, ARF has found itself lacking given ASEAN's reluctance to take sides in the dispute. The ADMM-Plus conducted an ambitious HADR exercise in Brunei in June 2013, but the aims and goals of the body have been kept relatively mundane, even as it seeks to avoid being called a talking shop.[131] ASEAN was perceived as slow to react to calamities in 2013 and 2014. In November 2013, Typhoon Haiyan struck the Philippines, leading to thousands of deaths. Asian countries worked at a bilateral level to help the Philippines. For example, Singapore's air force sent relief supplies to Tacloban and Cebu and extended the deployment of C-130 transports. Brunei dispatched a patrol vessel and fixed-wing aircraft. At the ASEAN level, however, the response materialised more slowly than that from countries outside the region. Having made HADR the centrepiece of its recent defence exercises, ASEAN failed to demonstrate its effectiveness when Haiyan struck.[132] Similarly, ASEAN's search-and-rescue (SAR) activities were of limited use following the disappearance of Malaysian Airlines flight MH370 in March 2014, a point made explicitly by Australia's defence minister at the 2014 Shangri-La Dialogue. The ADMM had conducted tabletop exercises in 2011, but they had not included SAR.[133] The EAS will also take some time to evolve from being merely a confidence-building institution to one that is armed with a thematic and problem-oriented agenda.[134] This has been labelled the 'Washington School' that promotes a functional or results-based approach to regionalism.[135]

The multitude of regional institutions has also become a duelling ground for China and US in their bids to win friends and influence people – what Shambaugh has called the 'balance of influence' in Asia.[136] In 2009, then-Australian Prime Minister Kevin Rudd told Hillary Clinton that his Asia-Pacific Community initiative sought to ensure that Chinese dominance at the EAS did not result in a 'Chinese Monroe Doctrine', and that China could succeed only if the US 'ceded the field'. As one Australian analyst put it, the US might not hold 'high ambitions' for what it can achieve at the EAS or other ASEAN institutions, but it can at the very least 'counter and restrict' China's freedom of movement within them.[137] At an ARF forum in July 2010, Clinton's statement that a multilateral diplomatic process should be used to settle the region's territorial disputes drew protests from the Chinese, who claimed Washington sought to intervene in its disputes with several ASEAN states over the South China Sea.

Beijing, for its part, wants regional bodies to exclude non-resident Asian powers such as the US. When Obama failed to attend the APEC summit in Bali and the EAS summit in Brunei in October 2013, Chinese leaders launched a charm offensive to remedy diplomatic missteps in the South China Sea and fine-tuned their policy towards ASEAN with economic carrots.[138] Although Obama's absence was due to a domestic crisis (the shutdown of the federal government over debt-servicing issues), a perception of on-again, off-again participation in the region's security institutions could make it difficult for Washington to sustain the rebalance to Asia.[139]

## A Concert of Asia

It has been argued that the region's security architecture is not capable of managing the simultaneous rise of China and perceived decline in American power. Thus two Australian academics, Coral Bell and Hugh White, have suggested the establishment of a 'Concert of Asia', drawing inspiration from the nineteenth-century Concert of Europe.[140] It would involve four powers – the US, China, Japan and Russia[141] – or perhaps only the first three.[142] More recently, White has suggested a four-power arrangement involving India instead of Russia, given the former's rise and the latter's declining footprint in Asia.[143]

A Concert of Asia could be built on the following elements: a willingness and commitment to resolve major-power conflict via negotiation, clear understandings about legitimate conduct, a focus on addressing common threats and a determination to insulate major powers' relations with each other from crises involving members outside the concert.[144]

A concert could address some of the most challenging problems in Asia's evolving geopolitical landscape. These include the US role in the region, how the rise of China is managed, and the role played by smaller powers. It might also portend some stability in the troubled Sino-Japanese relationship and would meet Japanese concerns that it be recognised as a great power in its own right. Given that the aim of a concert is to prevent the outbreak of crises or even conflict among the great powers, such an arrangement could, at least in theory, create conditions for the resolution of the disputes between China and Japan. Great-power collaboration would create such 'stabilising and convergent expectations that, when major problems arise, the major powers can sit down together to manage their differences'.[145] Indeed, this might be one of the most pressing tasks for a concert comprising, as White suggests, the US, China, Japan and India. A good outcome of this would be the implementation, by these four great powers, of arrangements that structurally improve Sino-Japanese relations – for example, Japanese apologies for its wartime atrocities and a Japanese admission of a dispute over the Senkaku/Diaoyu Islands.

There are doubts as to how a Concert of Asia would be established, and how well it would operate to prevent and solve crises. As White himself concedes, a stable Concert of Asia could emerge only when Japan is willing and able to act more independently of the US, so that it could join the concert in its own right.[146] A more pressing question is the way in which it might join such a concert. Given that Japan already has some strategic weight as the world's third-biggest economy, does Tokyo have to 'flick a switch' to actually declare itself a great power, and be accepted as such? As Ayson states, Japan needs to be accepted as part of a concert given its important role in Northeast Asia; that said, it does not strictly possess the attributes of a great power in terms of a United Nations Security Council seat or the possession of nuclear weapons, and there are restrictions in place on the Japanese military.[147] Secondly, the Japanese would feel a deep sense of ambivalence, and even apathy, towards a new role as a great power, given that they have enjoyed the benefits that came with the US–Japan alliance. In addition, younger Japanese do not favour their country playing a larger role in regional affairs.

Even if a concert were established, its efficacy could not be guaranteed. Given that the Chinese harbour fears about emerging Japanese militarism, they would not wish to see Japan embark on a strategically independent course or deviate from limitations on its military.[148] Chinese fears are shared by other Asian countries, albeit at a lesser intensity. As Singapore's elder statesman Lee Kuan Yew put it, Japan would not be able to play a leading political and security role in the region unless it squared its accounts from the last war. Allowing the JSDF abroad, he observed, is akin to 'giving a chocolate liqueur to an alcoholic', since there is no assurance that younger Japanese caught in a desperate situation might not 'set out with the same zeal as their grandfathers did'.[149]

A concert of great powers has been rejected outright by the smaller and emerging powers of Asia, in particular those in ASEAN. At a Sydney conference in 2008, a proposal by Australian Prime Minister Kevin Rudd to form a concert involving the Asia-Pacific's G20 members (Australia, China, India, Indonesia, Japan, Russia, South Korea and the United States) faced strong objections from some ASEAN countries. Tommy

Koh, a senior Singaporean diplomat, said that a 'directorate of one superpower and three major powers (the US, China, Japan and India) is an antiquated one which belongs to another time and another century'.[150]

## Notes

1. Thomas J. Christensen, 'China, the U.S.–Japan Alliance and the Security Dilemma in East Asia', *International Security*, vol. 23, no. 4, Spring 1999, pp. 49–50. The seminal work on the security dilemma is Robert Jervis, 'Cooperation under the Security Dilemma', *World Politics*, vol. 30, no. 2, January 1978, pp. 167–74.

2. Christensen, 'China, the U.S.–Japan Alliance and the Security Dilemma in East Asia', p. 51.

3. *Ibid.*, pp. 60–1.

4. Allen S. Whiting, *China Eyes Japan* (Berkeley, CA: University of California Press, 1989), pp. 129–30; Robert A. Manning, 'Burdens of the Past, Dilemmas of the Future: Sino-Japanese Relations in the Emerging International System', *Washington Quarterly*, vol. 17, no. 1, Winter 1994, pp. 45–8.

5. Zhao Quan Sheng, 'Chinese Foreign Policy in the Post-Cold War Era', *World Affairs*, vol. 159, no. 3, Winter 1997, pp. 116–18.

6. Interview in Beijing, August 2013.

7. Liu Jiangyong, 'New Trends in Sino–U.S.–Japan Relations', *Contemporary International Relations*, vol. 8, no. 7, July 1998, pp. 1–13, cited in Christensen, "China, the U.S.–Japan Alliance and the Security Dilemma in East Asia', p. 62.

8. Evelyn Goh, 'Japan, China and the Great Power Bargain in East Asia', EAI Fellow Program working paper no. 32 (Seoul: East Asia Institute, November 2011), pp. 7–8.

9. 'The Guidelines for Japan–U.S. Defense Cooperation', 1997, available at http://www.mofa.go.jp/region/n-america/us/security/guideline2.html.

10. US Information Agency, 'US–Japan Defense Cooperation Guidelines: Fears of a "Provoked" China, a "Remilitarized" Japan', *USIA Daily Digest*, 6 October 1997, available at http://www.fas.org/news/japan/97100601_rmr.html.

11. Japan Defense Agency, *Defense of Japan 2006*, http://www.mod.go.jp/e/publ/w_paper/2006.html, p. 222.

12. Richard C. Bush, *Perils of Proximity: China–Japan Security Relations* (Washington DC: Brookings Institution Press, 2010), loc. 524 (Kindle edition).

13. Ministry of Defense (China), China's National Defense in 2006, http://eng.mod.gov.cn/Database/WhitePapers/2006.htm.

14. Pan Yan, 'One Can Only Be Responsible To The Future When One Is Able To Deal With The Past Seriously', *Outlook Newsweek*, 11 April 2005, p. 11, cited in Yoshihide Soeya, David A. Welch and Masayaki Tadokoro, *Japan as a 'Normal Country'?: A Nation in Search*

*of Its Place in the World* (Toronto, Buffalo, London: University of Toronto Press, 2011), loc. 2556 (Kindle edition).

15 Information Office of the State Council, *The Diversified Employment of China's Armed Forces*, April 2013, available at http://news.xinhuanet.com/english/china/2013-04/16/c_132312681.htm.

16 Manning, 'Burdens of the Past', p. 52.

17 'The Japan, China, U.S. Triangle and East Asian Security. Symposium Report', *Japan Echo*, vol. 26, no. 3, June 1999, pp. 17–21.

18 Emma Chanlett-Avery, Kerry Dumbaugh and William H. Cooper, *Sino-Japanese Relations: Issues for U.S. Policy*, CRS Report for Congress R40093 (Washington DC: Congressional Research Service, 19 December 2008), p. 6.

19 Christopher Hughes, *Japan's Remilitarisation*, Adelphi 403 (London: International Institute for Strategic Studies, 2009), p. 28.

20 Ibid.

21 Ibid., p. 28.

22 The Council on Security and Defense Capabilities, *Japan's Vision for Future Security and Defense Capabilities*, October 2004, available at http://www.globalsecurity.org/wmd/library/news/japan/2004/041000-csdc-report.pdf.

23 Japan Defense Agency, *National Defense Program Guidelines, FY 2005–*, 10 December 2004, http://www.mod.go.jp/e/d_act/d_policy/pdf/national_guidelines.pdf.

24 *Defense of Japan 2006*, http://www.mod.go.jp/e/publ/w_paper/pdf/2006/1-2-2.pdf, p. 45.

25 *Defense of Japan 2006*, http://www.mod.go.jp/e/publ/w_paper/pdf/2006/1-2-3.pdf, pp. 48–9.

26 National Institute of Defense Studies, *East Asia Strategic Review 2008*, http://www.nids.go.jp/english/publication/east-asian/e2008.html, p. 103.

27 Ministry of Defence (Japan), *National Defence Program Outline 2010*, http://www.mod.go.jp/e/d_act/d_policy/pdf/guidelinesFY2011.pdf, pp. 2–3.

28 Ibid.

29 Martin Fackler, 'Japan Announces Defense Policy to Counter China', *New York Times*, 16 December 2010.

30 Ministry of Defense (Japan), *Defense of Japan 2013*, http://www.mod.go.jp/e/publ/w_paper/pdf/2013/07_Part1_Chapter0_Sec2.pdf, p. 3.

31 *Defense of Japan 2013*, http://www.mod.go.jp/e/publ/w_paper/pdf/2013/11_Part1_Chapter1_Sec3.pdf, p. 30.

32 Shinzo Abe, Keynote Address at the 2014 Shangri-La Dialogue, 30 May 2014, https://www.iiss.org/events/shangri la dialogue/archive/2014-c20c/opening-remarks-and-keynote-address-b0b2/keynote-address-shinzo-abe-a787.

33 Information Office of the State Council, *China's National Defense in 2010*, http://www.china.org.cn/government/whitepaper/node_7114675.htm.

34 Michael D. Swaine et al., *China's Military & the U.S.–Japan Alliance: A Strategic Net Assessment* (Washington DC: Carnegie Endowment for International Peace, 2013), p. 41; Anthony H. Cordesman, Ashley Hess and Nicholas S. Yarosh, *Chinese Military*

*Modernization and Force Development* (New York: Center for Strategic and International Studies, September 2013), p. 65, pp. 150–1; Andrew S. Erickson, 'China's Modernization of its Naval and Air Power Capabilities', in Ashley J. Tellis and Travis Tanner (eds), *Strategic Asia 2012–13: China's Military Challenge* (Washington DC: National Bureau of Asian Research, 2012).

35  Cordesman, Hess and Yarosh, *Chinese Military Modernization and Force Development*, pp. 150–1.

36  Erickson, 'China's Modernization of its Naval and Air Power Capabilities', p. 82.

37  Nan Li, 'The Evolution of China's Naval Strategy and Capabilities: From "Near Coast" and "Near Seas" to "Far Seas"', *Asian Security*, vol. 5, no. 2, 2009, pp. 144–69.

38  *Ibid.*, pp. 150–1.

39  Cordesman, Hess and Yarosh, *Chinese Military Modernization and Force Development*, pp. 150–1.

40  Li, 'The Evolution of China's Naval Strategy and Capabilities', p. 151.

41  Eric Sayers, 'The "Consequent Interest" of Japan's Southwestern Islands: A Mahanian Appraisal of the Ryukyu Archipelago', *Naval War College Review*, vol. 66, no. 2, Spring 2013, p. 55.

42  *Ibid.*

43  Toshi Yoshihara and James R. Holmes, *Red Star Over the Pacific* (Annapolis, MD: Naval Institute Press, 2010), pp. 66–7.

44  Data from the IISS Defence and Military Analysis Programme, 2014.

45  Office of the Secretary of Defense, *Military and Security Developments Involving the People's Republic of China 2013*, Annual Report to Congress, http://www.defense.gov/pubs/2013_china_report_final.pdf, p. 7.

46  Data from the IISS Defence and Military Analysis Programme, 2014.

47  *Ibid.*

48  Ronald O'Rourke, *China's Naval Modernization: Implications for U.S. Navy Capabilities – Background and Issues for Congress* (Washington DC: Congressional Research Service, 28 February 2014), p. 27.

49  Erickson, 'China's Modernization of its Naval and Air Power Capabilities', p. 68; Andrew S. Erickson, 'Chinese Anti-Ship Cruise Missile Firing as Part of Combined Anti-Carrier Exercises in East China Sea, 30 June–5 July', http://www.andrewerickson.com/2010/07/combined-arms-anti-ship-exercise-in-east-china-sea-30-june-5-july/, 6 July 2010.

50  James Holmes and Toshi Yoshihara, 'Ryukyu Chain in China's Island Strategy', *China Brief*, vol. 10, no. 19, 10 September 2010, p. 12.

51  Erickson, 'Chinese Anti-Ship Cruise Missile Firing as Part of Combined Anti-Carrier Exercises in East China Sea, 30 June–5 July'.

52  *Military and Security Developments Involving the People's Republic of China 2013*, p. 33.

53  *Defense of Japan 2013*, pp. 34–5.

54  Press Conference by Defense Minister Kitazawa, 17 December 2010, http://www.mod.go.jp/e/pressconf/2010/12/101217.html. The provisional English translation used the word 'vacant', but a better translation would have been 'vacuum' or 'power vacuum'. See David Fouse, *Japan's 2010 National Defense Program Guidelines: Coping*

*with Grey Zones* (Honolulu, HI: Asia-Pacific Center for Security Studies, April 2011), http://www.apcss.org/wp-content/uploads/2011/12/Fouse-Japan-Final.pdf.

55 Ministry of Defense (Japan), *Mid-Term Defense Program (FY2011–2015)*, http://www.mod.go.jp/e/d_act/d_policy/pdf/mid_termFY2011-15.pdf, p. 3.

56 'Japan Plans Troop Deployment Near Disputed Islands', *Nihon Keizai Shimbun*, 21 November 2010, cited in Fouse, 'Japan's 2010 National Defense Program Guidelines', p. 12.

57 *Mid-Term Defense Program (FY2011–2015)*, pp. 3–4.

58 Ministry of Defense (Japan), *Defense Posture Review Interim Report*, 2013, http://www.mod.go.jp/j/approach/agenda/guideline/2013_chukan/gaiyou_e.pdf.

59 *Ibid.*

60 Justin Goldman, 'An Amphibious Capability in Japan's Self-Defense Force', *Naval War College Review*, vol. 66, no. 4, October 2013, p. 119.

61 *Ibid.*

62 'Blunt Words and Keen Swords', *The Economist*, 10 November 2012; 'Japan, US to Cancel Island Drill: Report', Agence France-Presse, 19 October 2012; Mark McDonald, 'Despite Tensions, U.S. and Japan Begin a New Set of War Games', IHT Rendezvous blog, 4 November 2012, http://rendezvous.blogs.nytimes.com/2012/11/04/despite-tensions-u-s-and-japan-begin-a-new-set-of-war-games/.

63 Goldman, 'An Amphibious Capability in Japan's Self-Defense Force', p. 127; Isabel Reynolds, Takashi Hirokawa and Aki Ito,

'Japanese Troops Storm California Beach as Marine Power Eyed', Bloomberg.com, http://www.bloomberg.com/news/2013-07-10/japanese-troops-storm-california-beaches-as-marine-power-eyed.html, 11 July 2013.

64 'Japan–U.S. Amphibious Assault Drill Sends Message to China', *Nikkei Report*, 19 June 2013.

65 *Ibid.*; Trefor Moss, 'Japan's New (Defensive) Attack Force', *The Diplomat*, 3 November 2013, http://thediplomat.com/2013/11/03/japans-new-defensive-attack-force/.

66 Reynolds, Hirokawa and Ito, 'Japanese Troops Storm California Beach as Marine Power Eyed'.

67 Hiroshi Hiyama, 'Japan Putting Missiles on Pacific Gateway Islands', Agence France-Presse, 7 November 2013.

68 Terence. K. Kelly, Anthony Atler, Todd Nichols and Lloyd Thrall, *Employing Land-Based Anti-Ship Missiles in the Western Pacific* (Santa Monica, CA: RAND Corporation, 1 November 2013). See also Wendell Minnick, 'RAND Suggests Using Land-Based ASMs Against China', *Defense News*, 7 November 2013.

69 Holmes and Yoshihara, 'Ryukyu Chain in China's Island Strategy', pp. 11–14; National Institute of Defense Studies, *Japan: Towards the Establishment of a Dynamic Deterrence Force*, East Asia Strategic Review 201, p. 255, http://www.nids.go.jp/english/publication/east-asian/e2012.html; Eric Sayers, *Coastal Defense in Japan's Southwestern Islands: Force Posture Options for Securing Japan's Southern Flank*, Futuregram 13-001 (Arlington, VA: Project 2049 Institute, 7

January 2013), http://project2049.
net/documents/1301_ryukyu_
futuregram_sayers.pdf.

70  C. Fred Bergsten, Bates Gill,
Nicholas R. Lardy and Derek
Mitchell, *China: The Balance Sheet:
What the World Needs to Know Now
about the Emerging Superpower* (New
York: Public Affairs, 2006), p. 145.

71  *Ibid.*

72  'Tokyo Unveils New Carrier', *Global
Times*, 7 August 2013, http://www.
globaltimes.cn/content/802056.
shtml.

73  Paul Kallender-Umezu, 'Japan
Quietly Builds Limited Counter-A2/
AD Capabilities', *Defense News*, 17
September 2013.

74  'Comments: Chinese Navy Breaks
Through Island Chains Blockade',
*China Military*, 23 October 2013.

75  Hai Tao, 'The Chinese Navy has
a Long Way to Go to Get to the
Far Seas', *Guiji Xianqu Daobao*
(International Herald Leader),
6 January 2012, cited in Andrew
Berglund, '"Maneuver-5" Exercise
Focuses on Improving Distant
Seas Combat Capabilities', U.S.–
China Economic and Security
Review Commission Staff Report,
16 December 2013, available at
http://origin.www.uscc.gov/sites/
default/files/Research/Staff Report_
Maneuver-5 Exercise Focuses on
Improving Distant Seas Combat
Capabilities.pdf.

76  Hiyama, 'Japan Putting Missiles on
Pacific Gateway Islands'.

77  'Air Defense Identification Zone of
the P.R.C.', Xinhua, 23 November
2013.

78  Ministry of Foreign Affairs
(Japan), 'Press Conference by
Minister of Foreign Affairs Fumio

Kishida', 29 November 2013, http://
www.mofa.go.jp/press/kaiken/
kaiken4e_000024.html.

79  Lucy Hornby, 'China Attacks
Abe Air Defence Zone "Slander"
at ASEAN', *Financial Times*, 15
December 2013.

80  *Ibid.*

81  Ming Wan, *Sino-Japanese Relations:
Interaction, Logic and Transformation*
(Washington DC: Woodrow Wilson
Center Press, 2006), p. 44.

82  See, for example, James Holmes,
'The Top 5 Navies of the Indo-
Pacific', *The Diplomat*, 21 January
2013, http://thediplomat.com/the-
naval-diplomat/2013/01/21/the-
top-5-navies-of-the-indo-pacific/2/;
'China's Navy Seeks to "Wear Out"
Japanese Ships in Disputed Waters',
Reuters, 6 March 2013.

83  Peter Hays Gries, *China's New
Nationalism: Pride, Politics, and
Diplomacy* (Berkeley, CA: University
of California Press), loc. 212 (Kindle
edition).

84  International Crisis Group, *Dangerous Waters: China–Japan Relations on
the Rocks*, Asia Report no. 245 (Brussels: International Crisis Croup, 8
April 2013), pp. 17–18.

85  Robert Kelly, '4 Hypotheses on
Why China Suddenly Declared This
New Air Defense ID Zone', Asian
Security Blog, 29 November 2013,
http://asiansecurityblog.wordpress.
com/2013/11/29/4-hypotheses-on-
why-china-suddenly-declared-this-
new-air-defense-zone/.

86  International Crisis Group,
*Dangerous Waters*, p. 18.

87  James J. Przystup, 'Not Quite all
about Sovereignty – But Close',
*Pacific Forum CSIS Comparative
Connections*, vol. 6, no. 2, p. 124.

88 'DPJ Executive Wants SDF on Senkakus', *Japan Times*, 2 May 2005.

89 David Pilling, 'Japan's Culture Warriors Enlist an Emblem of the Imperial Past', *Financial Times*, 16 August 2013.

90 Reinhard Drifte, 'From "Sea of Confrontation" to "Sea of Peace, Cooperation and Friendship?" – Japan Facing China in the East China Sea', *Japan Aktuell*, March 2008, p. 14.

91 Ming Wan, *Sino-Japanese Relations*, pp. 145–6.

92 *Ibid.*, p. 146.

93 *Ibid.*, p. 143.

94 International Crisis Group, *Dangerous Waters*, pp. 27–8.

95 Interviews in Tokyo, September 2013.

96 *Ibid.*

97 Interview in Tokyo, September 2013.

98 Interview in Tokyo, September 2013.

99 International Crisis Group, *Dangerous Waters*, p. 49.

100 '"Secret" Japan–China Talks Held on Island Row: Report', Agence France-Presse, 15 October 2013.

101 International Crisis Group, *Dangerous Waters*, p. 14.

102 Patrick Ventrell, daily press briefing, US State Department, 30 August 2012, http://www.state.gov/r/pa/prs/dpb/2012/08/197078.htm.

103 Kor Kian Beng, 'China Wins Advantage in Air Defence Zone Dispute', *Straits Times*, 7 December 2013.

104 'Fact for Biden's Reference', *China Daily*, 4 December 2013.

105 Akira Kato, 'The United States: The Hidden Actor in the Senkaku Islands', *Asia Pacific Bulletin*, 2 April 2013, http://www.eastwestcenter.org/sites/default/files/private/apb205.pdf.

106 Paul J. Smith, 'The Senkaku/Diaoyu Island Controversy: A Crisis Postponed', *Naval War College Review*, vol. 66, no. 2, Spring 2013, pp. 39–40.

107 'Joint Press Availability with Japanese Foreign Minister Seiji Maehara', US State Department, 27 October 2010, http://www.state.gov/secretary/rm/2010/10/150110.htm.

108 'Abe "Snubbed" by Obama on Senkaku Issue: Chinese State Media', *Japan Times*, 25 February 2013.

109 Jonathan Eyal, 'American Policy Lost in Translation', *Straits Times*, 14 October 2013.

110 Mira Rapp-Hooper, 'An Ominous Pledge', *The Diplomat*, 26 September 2012.

111 Interviews in Beijing, August 2013. See also Gideon Rachman, 'A Gaffe-Prone Japan is a Danger to Peace in Asia', *Financial Times*, 13 August 2013. The article argues that a US security guarantee to Japan over the Diaoyu/Senkaku Islands could drag Washington into a war with China.

112 Patrick E. Tyler, 'As China Threatens Taiwan, It Makes Sure U.S. Listens', *New York Times*, 25 January 1996.

113 Rapp-Hooper, 'An Ominous Pledge'.

114 Jeffrey Smith, 'China Plans Manoeuvres Off Taiwan; Big Military Exercise Is Meant to Intimidate, U.S. Officials Say', *Washington Post*, 5 February 1996, p. A03.

115 Interviews in the UK, September 2013. See also Chee Mun Chew, 'China's Perspectives on the Major

Island Disputes in the East and South China Seas: Implications for the US's Strategic Balance towards Asia', research thesis, Air War College, Air University, Maxell AFB, 14 February 2013, http://www.au.af.mil/au/awc/awcgate/awc/2013_chew. pdf.

116 Helene Cooper, 'Hagel Spars with Chinese Over Islands and Security', *New York Times*, 8 April 2014.

117 Richard MacGregor and Jonathan Soble, 'Asian Diplomacy: Pivotal Moment', *Financial Times*, 21 April 2014.

118 Zbigniew Brzezinski, 'The Group of Two that Could Change the World', *Financial Times*, 13 January 2009.

119 Shai Oster, Andrew J. Nathan, Orville Schell, Susan Shirk, Tai Ming Cheung and John Delury, 'What's Really at the Core of China's "Core Interests"?', *China File*, 30 April 2013, http://www.chinafile.com/what-s-really-core-china-s-core-interests.

120 Michael Richardson, 'China's Changing Core Interests', *Straits Times*, 3 June 2013.

121 William Choong, *Moving Towards Empathy: A Study of Three Sino-American Deterrence Episodes in the 20th Century*, PhD dissertation, Australian National University.

122 See, for example, Zachary Keck, 'The Thucydides Trap and the Diaoyu/Senkaku Islands', *The Diplomat*, 10 July 2013.

123 Tom Donilon, 'The United States and the Asia-Pacific in 2013', Remarks at the Asia Society (New York), 11 March 2013.

124 Press Briefing on President Obama's Asia-Pacific Trip, 11 April 2014, Center for Strategic and International Studies, 11 April 2014, http://csis.org/files/attachments/0411CSIS-Press-Briefing.pdf.

125 Richard K. Betts, 'Wealth, Power and Instability: East Asia and the United States after the Cold War', *International Security*, vol. 18, no. 3, Winter 1993–94, pp. 34–77; Aaron L. Friedberg, 'Ripe for Rivalry: Prospects for Peace in Multipolar Asia', *International Security*, vol. 18, no. 3, Winter 1993–94, pp. 5–33.

126 Japan Center for International Exchange, *Towards Community Building in East Asia*, Dialogue and Research Monitor Overview Report, 2005, available at http://www.jcie.or.jp/drm.

127 Rodolfo C. Severino, 'Asean in Need of Stronger Cohesion', *Straits Times*, 9 December 2006.

128 Amitav Acharya, *Common Security with Asia: Changing Europe's Role from Model to Partner*, International Policy Analysis (Berlin: Freidrich Ebert Sifttung, December 2012), p. 3.

129 Graeme Dobell, 'The Platypus Design of Asia's Future', *The Diplomat*, 19 August 2013.

130 Zhang Tuosheng, 'Changes in China–Japan Relations and East Asia Security', in Ron Huisken (ed.), *The Architecture of Security in the Asia-Pacific* (Canberra: Australian National University Press, 2009), pp. 118–19.

131 Tan See Seng, 'A Farewell to Grandiosity? Practical Cooperation and the ADMM-Plus', *PacNet*, no. 65, 13 August 2013.

132 Euan Graham, 'Super Typhoon Haiyan: ASEAN's Katrina Moment?', PacNet, no. 82, 20 November 2013, https://csis.org/files/publication/Pac1382.pdf.

[133] Carl Thayer, 'Flight MH370 Shows Limits of Asean's Maritime Cooperation', *The Diplomat*, 18 March 2014, http://thediplomat.com/2014/03/flight-mh370-shows-limits-of-aseans-maritime-cooperation/.

[134] Ralf Emmers, Joseph Chinyong Liow and Tan See Seng, 'The East Asia Summit and the Regional Security Architecture', *Maryland Series in Contemporary Asian Studies*, no. 3, 2010, p. 50.

[135] Tan See Seng, 'Visions at War, EAS in the Regional Architecture Debate', *RSIS Commentaries*, no. 164, 10 November 2011.

[136] David Shambaugh, 'China Engages Asia: Reshaping the Regional Order', *International Security*, vol. 29, no. 3, Winter 2004/2005, pp. 64–99.

[137] William Choong, 'America to Play Role of China Watcher in East Asia Summit', *Straits Times*, 7 March 2011.

[138] Phuong Nguyen, 'China's Charm Offensive Signals a New Strategic Era in Southeast Asia', *CSIS Commentary*, 17 October 2013.

[139] 'Competitive Diplomacy in Southeast Asia', *IISS Strategic Comments*, vol. 19, no. 31, 21 October 2013, http://www.iiss.org/en/publications/strategic%20comments/sections/2013-a8b5/competitive-diplomacy-in-southeast-asia-aaa4.

[140] Coral Bell, *Living with Giants: Finding Australia's Place in a More Complex World* (Canberra: Australian Strategic Policy Institute, 2005); Coral Bell, *The End of the Vasco de Gama Era*, Lowy Institute Paper no. 21 (Sydney: Lowy Institute, 2007); Hugh White, *The China Choice: Why America Should Share Power* (Collingwood: Black Inc., 2012) (Kindle edition).

[141] Amitav Acharya, 'A Concert of Asia?', *Survival*, vol. 41, no. 3, Autumn 1999, p. 98.

[142] Douglas Stuart, 'Towards a Concert of Asia', *Asian Survey*, vol. 31, no. 3, March 1997, p. 241.

[143] White, *The China Choice*, locs 1853–87 (Kindle edition).

[144] *Ibid.*, locs 1809–31 (Kindle edition); Malcolm Cook, Raoul Heinrichs, Rory Medcalf and Andrew Shearer, *Power and Choice: Asian Security Futures* (Sydney: Lowy Institute for International Policy, June 2010), pp. 40–2.

[145] Robert Ayson, 'The Six Party Talks Process: Towards an Asian Concert?', in Huisken (ed.), *The Architecture of Security in the Asia-Pacific*, p. 62.

[146] White, *The China Choice*, locs 1880–2 (Kindle edition).

[147] Ayson, 'The Six Party Talks Process', p. 63.

[148] Kenneth Pyle, *Japan Rising: The Resurgence of Japanese Power and Purpose* (New York: Public Affairs, 2007), locs 7087–8 (Kindle edition).

[149] Ang Cheng Guan, *Lee Kuan Yew's Strategic Thought* (Abingdon: Routledge, 2013), p. 75.

[150] Tommy Koh, 'Who Will Lead Asia', *Straits Times*, 29 September 2012.

The dispute between Japan and China over the Senkaku/Diaoyu Islands, which is entangled with a dispute over Japan's conduct in the period 1895–1945, has led to the prepositioning of military forces in and around the disputed islands, and raised the possibility of open conflict. At the strategic level, there is a vicious cycle at work – the more Japan refuses to come clean on historical issues and admit that there is a dispute over the islands, the more China feels compelled to act, in the form of incursions to the waters surrounding the islands. Top-level dialogue and interactions between political leaders from both sides have largely disappeared.

Existing trends entail an appreciable risk of armed conflict. The US rebalance to the Asia-Pacific is stoking Chinese fears about containment and Japan casting off its post-war restrictions in order to become a 'normal power'. In the absence of any move by Japan to recognise that a territorial dispute exists, China will continue or increase its maritime incursions into the territorial waters of the Senkakus/Diaoyus. The Japan Coast Guard will respond by intercepting Chinese vessels. At some point, another 'radar lock-on' incident could occur, leading to military exchanges. This would draw in the US, because the disputed islands are covered by the US security guarantee to Japan. That in turn would imperil regional stability.

More optimistic scenarios are conceivable. If the Chinese and Japanese authorities recognise the dangers of the current course, they could agree to take measures aimed at reducing tensions and limiting the diplomatic and strategic impact of the disputes over history and the islands. This would include the creation of crisis-management mechanisms, a code of conduct in the East China Sea and political understandings to lower the tensions over the islands and historical issues through shelving or a similar arrangement.

There could also be a more encompassing settlement between China and Japan, in which the two states would reach an agreement on historical issues, while Japan would help China to play a greater role in regional stability, for example through participation in the East Asia Summit. This could happen in parallel with the further development of regional security institutions. If the US and China formed a G2, dividing the region into spheres of influence, it would fundamentally alter the Senkaku/Diaoyu dispute, most likely to the benefit of China. This would not guarantee stability: a weakened Japan might conclude that it had little choice but to explore negotiations with China, although it is also possible that Tokyo might respond to the withdrawal of US protection by adopting a more forthright foreign policy and defence posture that stressed the importance of defending territorial integrity in the face of any challenge. Even if Japan were minded to seek an accommodation with China, the establishment of a G2 might create expectations in Beijing that ranged well beyond what Tokyo was willing to concede.

## Tackling the causes

Both states will have to act to ensure that current tensions do not escalate to military conflict, and to put relations on track to one of the more positive scenarios outlined above. The possibilities can be ranked according to ambition: measures to tackle the roots of the dispute, and measures to treat the symptoms.

Tackling the roots of the dispute would require China and Japan to engage in negotiations or refer the case to binding arbitration. (Even a Japanese expression of readiness to take the dispute to the International Court of Justice would represent a *de jure* acknowledgement of the dispute and would elicit a rejection by China, which has stressed that the islands are part of Chinese territory.[1]) They would concurrently have to develop relations less beholden to domestic nationalist impulses, with historical issues to be settled by an apology acceptable to both sides.

### Burying the hatchet

In 2003, Chinese journalist Ma Licheng published an essay, 'New Thinking on Relations with Japan', that called for Beijing to adopt a more enlightened approach to Tokyo for the sake of long-term relations. Ma, an editorial writer with the *People's Daily*, took issue with xenophobic tendencies among his compatriots. He dwelt upon the difficulties suffered by Long Yongtu, the vice trade minister who was accused by domestic critics of being a traitor for negotiating China's WTO entry in 1999. To Ma, Chinese perceptions that the US was using the instrument of globalisation to enslave China, and calls for China to isolate its economy from the outside world, heralded a return to the spirit of the Boxer Rebellion around the turn of the nineteenth century.[2] Looking to Japan, Ma said that it would be impossible to prevent 'a defeated country from restoring its normal country status'. Thus China should be 'psychologically prepared' for Japan to revert to becoming a 'political and military major power again'.[3] His prescriptions were straightforward: China, as a great power itself, should not be 'too harsh' on Japan. Tokyo had apologised for its conduct and had underlined its sincerity by providing substantial financial aid to China. Both sides should adopt a forward-looking approach to their relationship and push for a collection of free-trade zones in the Asia-Pacific.[4]

Ma's essay drew support from Shi Yinhong, an academic from Renmin University. Shi recommended that China and Japan pursue rapprochement to balance against the US.[5] Thus China should put less stress on questions of history and accept Japanese apologies, while supporting Tokyo's bid for a permanent seat on the UN Security Council and downplaying accusations that Japan was turning to militarism. These steps, Shi added, would strengthen China in its relations with the US.[6] In two subsequent articles, Shi stressed that the Chinese approach to Japan should not be based on emotions, but on the logic of strategic relations.[7]

The proposals of Ma and Shi were widely derided. Ma received death threats and retired early from *People's Daily*,[8] while Shi was called a 'quack' for doling out prescriptions without a clear diagnosis.[9] A series of incidents in 2003 and 2004 highlighted how little prescriptions were taken to heart by ordinary Chinese. In June 2003, Internet activists organised the first-ever mainland Chinese trip to the Diaoyu Islands.[10] Even Chinese moderates, who had called for balance in the Sino-Japanese relationship, argued that the most significant weakness of Shi's prescription was the failure to take into account Japan's grand strategy. With Japan a US ally primed to hedge against China's rise, it was near-impossible for China and Japan to achieve genuine cooperation similar to that between Germany and France.[11]

In Japan, too, there have been proposals for a strategic rapprochement. When the DPJ came to power in 2009, it called for an 'equal alliance' with the US and a more autonomous foreign policy that emphasised relations with Asia, particularly China.[12] Prime Minister Yukio Hatoyama proposed to Chinese President Hu Jintao that the East China Sea should become a 'sea of fraternity instead of a sea of disputes'.[13] Hatoyama's proposal for a European Union-like East Asian Community (EAC) centred on Northeast Asia was warmly welcomed in Beijing.[14] The US viewed the EAC proposal sceptically, seeing it as tantamount to Japan acquiescing to a China-centric regional system that would undercut American primacy in the Asia-Pacific.[15] In December 2009, DPJ Secretary-General Ichiro Ozawa led a 600-strong delegation to China and, together with Hu, pledged to deepen party-to-party ties by holding dialogues, enhancing trust and seeking common development.[16] (This goodwill dissipated ten months later after the incident in which a Chinese fishing trawler rammed JCG vessels near the Senkakus/Diaoyus.)

It is worth noting that the proposals within China for a more constructive approach to Japan were ridiculed even before the territorial dispute reached its current level of acrimony. The prospects for a step change in China's approach in 2014–15, under the leadership of the assertive Xi Jinping, are small. Japanese analysts note that Xi has been receptive to Foreign Minister Yang Jiechi's suggestion that Japan could be isolated. Before his ascent to power in late 2012, Xi had taken on a more hardline position towards Japan; any conciliatory initiatives towards Japan by Hu and Premier Wen Jiabao were criticised by Xi's allies.[17]

Chinese analysts believe it will be several years before a pro-China politician like Hatoyama could rise to power in Japan.[18] Moreover, any rapprochement would be hampered by a disagreement between China and Japan over their future roles in the region. China does not accept Japan's bid to play a secure and honourable place in Asia's emerging political order. In Japanese eyes, China is going down the same militarist route Japan took in the 1930s by allowing the military to break free from civilian control and to challenge American power in the Pacific.[19]

## Tackling history

Chinese and Japanese analysts agree that joint research on historical issues would benefit the Sino-Japanese relationship. Some steps have been taken in this direction, such as the agreement between Abe and Hu to a joint historical study by academics from both countries.[20] Another ground-breaking project was *The Modern and Contemporary History of Three East Asian Countries*, started by 50 independent teachers, historians and members of civic groups from China, Japan and South Korea. The 2005 work was the first joint history textbook in East Asia, and took 11 meetings, six revisions and three years to complete.[21] Critics complain that the book has done nothing to change China's official narrative on history, but Wang argues that the work is an 'important first step' to approach sensitive historical issues in East Asia, particularly with its acknowledgement of multiple perspectives.[22]

The establishment of a common understanding of the historical record would go a long way to repairing damaged relations. Yet even that endeavour can fall victim to politics. In 2001, South Korean President Kim Dae-jung and Japanese Prime Minister Junichiro Koizumi established the Japan–ROK History Research Committee, a state-sponsored effort to come up with a reconciled view of the past.[23] Although the project adopted a UNESCO model of writing a parallel history, the two sides failed to come to a consensus on what should be incorporated into the textbooks. They disagreed over how to interpret Japan's colonial rule, including its role (or lack thereof) in Korea's modernisation. In 2010, another report failed to reach consensus on Japan's colonial rule.[24]

A similar China–Japan effort to write a parallel history of 2,000 years of bilateral relations ran into problems concerning which topics to focus on – the Chinese were more interested in the colonial and wartime periods, while the Japanese were keen to focus on the post-war era.[25] A final report was made public in January 2010, only to reveal that the two sides could not resolve differences on controversial events such as the 1937 Nanjing Massacre.[26]

*Managing nationalistic impulses*

One cause of the deterioration in bilateral relations between 2010 and 2014 was the fact that the Chinese and Japanese governments are beholden to nationalist constituencies. This is particularly true for China, where nationalist and anti-Japanese sentiment is broadly based. It is in the interest of the Chinese authorities to restrain anti-Japanese sentiment because it can be turned into opposition against the Chinese government.[27] The CCP has sought to co-opt and suppress Diaoyu activism, out of fear that such activism can threaten the party's legitimacy.[28]

Such measures, however, are difficult for the Chinese government, given that China has traditionally exploited historical issues for strategic gain at the expense of Japan.[29] They would, too, be deeply unpopular. In 2012, 70 of 200 prime-time dramas on major television networks were about the Sino-Japanese war, a reflection of popular sentiment among the Chinese people.[30] New textbooks approved after 1992 blamed the West (and Japan) for China's past sufferings. Narratives about 'China as victor' were slowly replaced by 'China as victim' in nationalist discourse. The overarching goal was to redirect the anger of young Chinese people away from the CCP.[31] Such an entrenched policy of the party would be hard to reverse.

In Japan, restraint of nationalist elements is tied up with the role that the Yasukuni memorial plays in national life. Japan could seek to honour its wartime veterans at a new and secular memorial. Some Japanese moderates have suggested that national ceremonies be held at the Chidorigafuchi National Cemetery, Japan's tomb of the unknown soldier.[32] Prime Minister Yasuo Fukuda, aware of Chinese and South Korean sensitivities, visited it in 2008. More recently, US Secretary of State John Kerry and US Secretary of Defense Chuck Hagel visited Chidorigafuchi, in what was interpreted as an encouragement to Japan's government to avoid the Yasukuni Shrine.[33] For similar reasons US President Barack Obama visited the Meiji Shrine in 2014.

Putting a stop to Yasukuni visits by Japanese politicians would help to diffuse Korean and Chinese anger over issues of history. Fukuda's declaration that he would not visit the shrine was viewed positively by China and South Korea. However, the likelihood that Abe will eschew Yasukuni is low. He visited the shrine in December 2013 and followed up with a ceremonial tree offering in April 2014. In that month, 147 legislators visited Yasukuni, including some from Abe's LDP. Abe has repeatedly said that he regretted not visiting the shrine during his first term as prime minister in 2006–07. He said that his critics misunderstood his intentions, which were to pay respect to those who lost their 'previous lives' for Japan.[34]

It would not be easy politically for Abe and the LDP to cut their ties to Yasukuni. The electoral base constituency of Japan's conservative party still feels an intimate sense of bereavement for the 2m soldiers who died in the Second World War. Understandably, such a constituency is hostile to any condemnation of Japanese war crimes that denies honour and respect

to those who died for their country.[35] Abe's foreign-policy
inclinations are influenced heavily by former prime minister
Nobusuke Kishi, his maternal grandfather. During his premier-
ship, between 1957 and 1960, Kishi sought to revise Japan's
1947 Constitution, to make Japan an equal partner of the US
and to conduct a more muscular diplomacy.[36] By encouraging
a spirit of nationalism, Abe hopes to instill self-confidence and
patriotism. This involves what he terms a 'departure from the
post-war regime' – that is, from the judgments of the Tokyo
War Crimes Tribunal, Tokyo's subservience to the US and
the need for continued contrition towards China and South
Korea.[37] The combination of such historical revisionism and
a values-oriented 'assertive diplomacy', centred on forming
a coalition of like-minded countries based on values such as
democracy and human rights, is the product of Japan's wartime
trauma and its subsequent experience of occupation, which
has resulted in Japan's loss of true 'independence'. By arguing
for a reinterpretation of the constitution, Abe hopes to regain
'independence' for the country.[38] This would be tantamount to
a revolution in post-war Japanese diplomacy and more importantly, a move against an international regime based on the San
Francisco system built and led by the United States.[39]

*A mutually acceptable apology*
Apologies have to be made and accepted for reconciliation to
work.[40] The current climate is hardly conducive to this: China
continues to insist that Japan make a full, sincere apology,
while Japan believes that it already has done so and suspects
that China is using the issue to gain an advantage.

One way out of this impasse is for Japanese officials to
continue to offer apologies for the country's wartime atrocities. A good example is the expression of remorse offered by
Defense Minister Itsunori Onodera at the 2013 Shangri-La

Dialogue. Onodera invoked the spirit of the 1995 statement by then-Prime Minister Tomiichi Murayama, stating that Japan had 'caused tremendous damage and suffering to the people of many countries'. A further step would be to ensure that Japanese politicians do not incite China by making controversial statements about matters of history. One example was the April 2013 statement by Abe, when he appeared to question whether Japan had actually 'invaded' China during the Second World War.[41]

Beijing has not directly asked Japan to apologise in the manner of former German Chancellor Willy Brandt, who in 1970 knelt down in front of a memorial dedicated to Jews killed in the war and expressed remorse for the suffering inflicted on the people of Poland and other European countries. However, such an act would go a long way to meeting Chinese wishes. Speaking to journalists in October 2012, Vice Foreign Minister Zhang Zhijun said that Brandt's 'sincere' act of contrition was 'very important' in terms of reconciliation between Germany and other European countries.[42] In February 2014, Chinese state television showed footage of Brandt's apology. This set the stage for Xi to draw a contrast between Germany's historical contrition and Japan's apparent lack.[43]

Abe is unlikely to contemplate a Brandt-style apology. He and his allies feel that Japan has already apologised, and that demands for further contrition fail to acknowledge all the good that Japan has done since the Second World War.[44] The LDP's electoral base is hostile to any confession of Japanese war crimes.[45] There is also a fundamental difference between Japan's Confucian 'shame culture' and Germany's 'guilt culture'. The former frowns upon confessions of wrong, given that 'shame is a major sanction'. Shame cannot be relieved, as guilt can be, by confession and atonement.[46] Finally, a Brandt-style apology would have deep ramifications domestically because, whereas Germany built its post-war institutions from scratch, Japan retained the emperor. An apology in the mould of Brandt's would undermine the post-war system, endorsed by the US, that enabled Japan to rise after 1945.[47]

## Treating the symptoms

Structural impediments and an absence of political will militate against tackling the root causes of the China–Japan dispute, but there is still some scope for actions by both sides to avoid confrontations of the kind that risk an outbreak of conflict.

### Shelving revisited

Although the Japanese government refuses to acknowledge that there was an agreement to shelve the dispute in the 1970s, there is plenty of evidence suggesting that such an understanding was observed (see Chapter 2). One option would be to tacitly restore the shelving arrangement. A second approach would be for Japan and China to agree on a form of words that allowed both sides to defend (to their own publics) their core interests. If it accepted that there was a 'difference of opinion' or 'a contention' over the islands, the Japanese government could argue that it had not admitted to the existence of a dispute and retain administration of the islands, while China's government could demonstrate to the public some progress towards eventual restitution. Japan could then reduce coast-guard patrols around the islands while China's authorities would work to prevent maritime incursions by state bodies or citizens. This would give the two states some space to focus on mutual interests in the commercial sphere.[48]

A back-room agreement to return to the 1970s' tacit understanding would yield quick dividends for bilateral relations. In practice, however, deferral of the dispute would run into various challenges. Firstly, Japanese officials have doggedly refused to acknowledge the dispute. Speaking to the *Straits Times* in an interview in January 2013, Foreign Minister Fumio Kishida – through an English interpreter – referred to the 'territorial dispute of [the] Senkakus'. Kishida's minders quickly corrected him, saying that the minister was referring to the 'issue related to the Senkaku Islands'.[49] According to one analyst in Japan, the government has deliberately destroyed records of the 1972 Tanaka–Zhou conversation about the islands. This was admitted to by Hiroshi Hashimoto, head of the China Division in the Foreign Ministry, in an interview in 2000.[50] Secondly, there is growing sentiment in political circles, the media and the academic community in Japan that the government should take a firmer stance against China as it pertains to territorial issues.[51] Thirdly, if Japan were to concede that there was a dispute, it would reward China's coercive tactics and encourage a similar approach in the future.

*Crisis management*

In the context of a desire on both sides to reduce tensions, China and Japan could undertake various crisis-management and confidence-building arrangements. In the past five years, the two states have sought to develop various maritime confidence-building and communication arrangements. These include the Japan–China Maritime Communications Mechanism (JCMCM), the Maritime Search and Rescue (SAR) Cooperation Agreement and the High-Level Consultation on Maritime Affairs (High-Level Consultation).[52] The JCMCM is primarily a military-to-military agreement and analogous to the United States–China Maritime Consultative Agreement. It is primarily a mechanism for communication between the militaries of the two countries. The SAR agreement is a 30-year-old effort which constitutes a 'concrete step to make the East China Sea a "Sea of Peace, Cooperation and Friendship"'. The

High-Level Consultation was agreed upon by Wen Jiabao and Japanese Prime Minister Yoshihiko Noda.[53] It serves as a 'platform for increasing dialogue and communication, promoting cooperating and managing disputes at sea'. In January 2014, the Japanese foreign minister proposed that China and Japan establish an emergency hotline between their capitals.[54] The proposal, however, gained no traction given the poor relations between the two countries. The usefulness of such mechanisms remains to be seen.[55]

After the 2010 boat collision incident, China and Japan also began to negotiate a separate communications mechanism involving various layers, including law-enforcement agencies, militaries and foreign ministries. According to reports in Japan, Tokyo also indicated to Beijing that future Chinese protesters on the islands would be arrested and then deported rather than jailed, provided that there were no aggravating circumstances. China meanwhile indicated that it would seek to prevent protesters from leaving Chinese harbours in their vessels. Both governments denied such an understanding was in fact reached,[56] but if that is the case, it is conceivable that an arrangement on similar lines could be agreed in future. If China can reduce the number of maritime incursions into the territorial and contiguous waters of the islands, and Japan the intensity and frequency of its coast-guard patrols, it would help to reduce the operational fatigue of the maritime agencies on both sides. After all, a Japanese expert says, such incursions and patrols are 'meaningless'.[57]

While crisis-management measures sound plausible in theory, their execution depends on effective, open channels of communication between Beijing and Tokyo. These are not a given. In April 2014, for example, it was reported that Admiral Katsutoshi Kawana, the chief of staff of the JMSDF, was to meet his PLAN counterpart, Admiral Wu Shengli on the sidelines of the Western Pacific Naval Symposium (WPNS) in Qingdao. If it had materialised, the meeting would have been the first time the two nations' top naval officers had met in five years.[58] After the symposium, however, the PLAN denied that any such meeting had taken place. The two navy chiefs had only shared a brief chat and agreed 'on the importance of the code of behaviour'. This was a reference to the WPNS's Code for Unplanned Encounters at Sea (CUES), a proposal tabled ten years earlier and finally approved by navy chiefs from countries represented at the symposium, including China, Japan, the Philippines and the US. The code defines ways for naval ships and aircraft to manoeuvre and communicate when they meet 'casually or unexpectedly'.[59] While Wu said that CUES was 'highly significant to navies in the region' in promoting communication and reducing misjudgement, China's Defence Ministry did not clarify whether it would abide by the code in the South China Sea and East China Sea, where China has territorial claims. At the symposium, Fan Changlong, the vice chairman of the Central Military Commission, told delegates that China would not 'swallow the bitter pill' of ceding its sovereign rights to other countries.[60] This reflects the fact that China will not agree to crisis-management accords that restrict its ability to assert its rights to disputed territories.

A more viable proposal is China's 'Three "No"s' – no entry into disputed waters, no landings on the islands and no overflight by either state.[61] It would be easier for both states to agree to restrict certain activities – such as overflight and entry into the islands – rather than trying to craft a new agreement from scratch. There are some grounds for believing that China is open to such an arrangement. According to one analysis, Chinese patrols within the 12nm territorial waters around the Senkakus/Diaoyus dropped steeply from as many as four a week before October 2013 to an average of one a week thereafter.[62] The reduction could signal China's willingness not to escalate the dispute with Japan further, and is consistent with China's apparent bargaining position that Japanese recognition that there is a dispute could lead to a de-escalation of Chinese activity around the islands.[63]

## The art of the possible

A possible first step would be for the two states to agree crisis-management measures such as hotlines and an incident-at-sea agreement. The latter would serve a dual purpose: reducing the risk that accidental clashes might escalate into something more serious, and establishing a foundation for further dialogue. An incident-at-sea agreement between the US and the Soviet Union in 1972 all but eliminated unsafe and unprofessional conduct between their navies.[64] A similar agreement, or even adoption of the less ambitious International Regulations for Preventing Collisions at Sea (signed between the US and China) or a CUES could be useful in reducing the risk of miscalculation. A second step would be for China and Japan to return to the tacit understanding that the dispute would be shelved. Such a return does not have to be made public. This would create the space for bilateral relations to develop some momentum and trust in other areas.

Achieving political understanding between Beijing and Tokyo will not be easy, but continuing with the current course would be an exercise in folly. Economic and commercial ties between the two countries do not preclude the possibility of war.[65] The policy stances of China, Japan and the US are largely set. Japan refuses to admit that there is a dispute, and is determined to defend its sovereign territory. China perceives that Japan has departed from the 1970s shelving arrangement and, mindful that by 2022 Tokyo will have demonstrated 50 years of control over the Senkakus/Diaoyus, feels it has little choice but to challenge Japan's hold over the islands in order to support its own sovereignty claim. The US is at pains to stress that it has no position in the dispute, but it is tethered to Japan by a security guarantee that covers the islands.

As Barbara Tuchman has noted, there are many examples throughout history of states that pursued ruinous policies that ran contrary to their interests. Sweden under Charles XII, France under Napoleon and Germany under Hitler all invaded Russia despite the disasters suffered by their predecessors; Britain's George III opted to coerce rather than conciliate the American colonies, despite advice from his counsellors to the contrary.[66] A conflict between Japan and China over a handful of tiny islands would be baffling to any student schooled in the notion that states are rational actors guided by their interests. Yet it remains a distinct possibility.

## Notes

1 Michael Green, 'Sino-Japanese Tensions: The Case for Strategic Patience', *Lowy Interpreter*, 31 October 2013, http://www.lowyinterpreter.org/post/2013/10/31/Sino-Japanese-tensions-The-case-for-strategic-patience.aspx.

2 Ma Licheng, 'Duiri guanxi xinsi' (New Thinking on Relations with Japan), *Zhanlue yu guanli*, no. 6, 2002, pp. 41, 45.

3 *Ibid.*, p. 43.

4 *Ibid.*, p. 47.

5 Shi Yinhong, 'Zhongri jiejin yu waijiao geming' (Sino-Japanese Rapprochement and the 'Diplomatic Revolution'), *Zhanlue yu guanli*, no. 2, 2003, pp. 71–2.

6 *Ibid.*, pp. 71–5.

7 Shi Yinhong, 'Lishi wenti yu da zhanlue quanheng' (The History Question and the Great Strategic Balance), *Kangri zhanzheng yanjiu* (Journal of the War of Resistance Against Japan), no. 3, 2003, pp. 191–5; Shi Yinhong, 'Guanyu zhongri guanxi zhanlue sikao' (Strategic Thinking in Sino-Japanese Relations), *Shije jingji zhengzhi* (World Economics and Politics), no. 9, 2003, pp. 10–11, cited in Peter Hays Gries, 'China's "New Thinking" on Japan', *China Quarterly*, no. 184, December 2005, pp. 839–40.

8 Gries, 'China's New Thinking', pp. 838–9.

9 Wang Jianwei, 'Chinese Discourse on Japan as a "Normal Country"',

in Yoshihide Soeya, David A. Welch and Masayaki Tadokoro (eds), *Japan as a 'Normal Country'?: A Nation in Search of Its Place in the World* (Toronto, Buffalo, London: University of Toronto Press, 2011), loc. 2766 (Kindle edition).

10 Ching Cheong, 'Chinese Public Speaks Up on Japanese Ties', *Straits Times*, 24 November 2003; Isao Yamamoto, 'Japan Urgently Needs to Rethink Nature of Relationship with China', *Nikkei Weekly*, 17 November 2003; Gries, 'China's New Thinking', pp. 833–4.

11 'Some Recommendations on Improving China–Japan Relations', *Contemporary International Relations* no. 6, 2004, p. 9, cited in Wang, 'Chinese Discourse on Japan as a "Normal Country"', p. 135.

12 Tetsuo Kotani, 'Turbulent Changes: The Democratic Party Government and Japan's Foreign Policy', *Russia in Global Affairs*, December 2010, http://eng.globalaffairs.ru/number/Turbulent-Changes-15082; Daniel Sneider, 'The New Asianism: Japanese Foreign Policy under the Democratic Party of Japan', *Asia Policy*, no. 12, July 2011, pp. 99–129.

13 Sachiko Sakamaki, 'China's Hu, Japan's Hatoyama Agree to Extend Thaw in Relations', Bloomberg.com, 22 September 2009, http://www.bloomberg.com/apps/news?pid=newsarchive&sid=amN_cwK8u4NU.

14 Goh Sui Noi, 'Shaping a New East Asia', *Straits Times*, 11 November 2009.

15 Sneider, 'The New Asianism', p. 111.

16 'Ruling Parties of China, Japan Agree on Seeking Stronger Overall Relationship', Xinhua, 11 December 2009.

17 Interviews in Tokyo, September 2013.

18 Interviews in Beijing, August 2013.

19 Gideon Rachman, 'China and Japan are Heading for a Collision', *Financial Times*, 18 November 2013.

20 Wang, 'Chinese Discourse on Japan as a "Normal Country"', in Soeya, Welch and Tadokoro (eds), *Japan as a 'Normal Country'?*, loc. 2839 (Kindle edition).

21 Zheng Wang, *Never Forget National Humiliation: Historical Memory in Chinese Politics and Foreign Relations* (New York: Columbia University Press, 2012), locs. 4333–409 (Kindle edition).

22 *Ibid.*, loc. 4409 (Kindle edition).

23 Shin Gi-Wook, 'National Identities, Historical Memories, and Reconciliation in Northeast Asia', *The Asan Forum*, 25 January 2014, http://www.theasanforum.org/national-identities-historical-memories-and-reconciliation-in-northeast-asia/.

24 *Ibid.*

25 *Ibid.*

26 *Ibid.*; 'New Joint Study Fails to Bridge Divide Between Japan and China on Nanjing', Agence France-Presse, 1 February 2010.

27 International Crisis Group, *Dangerous Waters: China–Japan Relations on the Rocks*, Asia Report no. 245 (Brussels: ICG, 8 April 2013), p. 19, n. 127; Peh Shing Huei, 'Give Credit Where It's Due', *Straits Times*, 28 March 2011.

28 Peter Hays Gries, *China's New Nationalism: Pride, Politics, and Diplomacy* (Berkeley, CA: University

of California Press, 2004), loc. 1520 (Kindle edition).

29 Heng Yee Kuang, 'Japan: Troublemaker or Troubleshooter?', *Straits Times*, 25 March 2014.

30 'Analysis: Anti-Japan Dramas the Last Refuge of China's Cornered Film-Makers', BBC Monitoring, 10 July 2013.

31 Wang, *Never Forget National Humiliation*, pp. 100–2.

32 Jennifer Lind, 'The Perils of Apology', *Foreign Affairs*, vol. 88, no. 3, May–June 2009, pp. 132–46.

33 'Kerry at Japanese Cemetery in Apparent US Yasukuni Push', Agence France-Presse, 3 October 2013.

34 George Nishiyama, 'Abe Visit to Controversial Shrine Draws Rare U.S. Criticism', *Wall Street Journal*, 26 December 2013.

35 John Dower, *Ways of Forgetting, Ways of Remembering: Japan in the Modern World* (New York: New Press, 2012), loc. 1635 (Kindle edition).

36 William Choong, 'Stoking Old Flames in New Japan', *Straits Times*, 7 January 2013.

37 Kosuke Takahashi, 'Shinzo Abe's Nationalist Strategy', *The Diplomat*, 13 February 2014.

38 Yoshihide Soeya, 'A "Normal" Middle Power: Interpreting Changes in Japanese Security Policy in the 1990s and After', in Soeya, Welch and Tadokoro, *Japan as a 'Normal Country'?*, loc. 1499 (Kindle edition).

39 *Ibid.*, loc. 1499 (Kindle edition).

40 Thomas U. Berger and Bong Youngshik, 'To Apologize and To Forgive: Lessons for Asia from Europe's Struggle with History', Issue Brief no. 34, Asan Institute for Policy Studies, 22 November 2012, p. 2.

41 Toko Sekiguchi, 'Japanese PM Stokes Wartime Passions', *Wall Street Journal*, 25 April 2013, http://online.wsj.com/news/articles/SB10001424127887324743704578444273613265696.

42 'Vice Foreign Minister Zhang Zhijun Gave Briefing to Chinese and Foreign Journalists on the Diaoyu Dao Issue (Transcript)', 27 October 2012, http://www.fmprc.gov.cn/eng/topics/diaodao/t983015.shtml.

43 'China, Eyeing Japan, Seeks WW2 Focus for Xi During Germany Visit', Reuters, 23 February 2014.

44 Interviews in Tokyo, September 2013.

45 Dower, *Ways of Forgetting*, loc. 1619 (Kindle edition).

46 See Ian Buruma, *The Wages of Guilt: Memories of War in Germany and Japan* (New York: Farrar Straus Giroux, 1994), p. 116. Buruma was citing Ruth Benedict's classic *Chrysanthemum and the Sword*. However, he did not accept it outright, given the fact that there are too many exceptions. For example, there are Germans who do not have the 'slightest wish' to confess; as for the Japanese, many have gone to China to make amends.

47 Interviews in Tokyo, September 2013. A March 2013 feature film, entitled *Emperor* and starring American actor Tommy Lee Jones, dwells on the issue of whether the American occupation forces in Japan should find the emperor guilty of war crimes.

48 Interviews in Beijing and Tokyo, August and September 2013.

49  William Choong, 'Let Wisdom Prevail Over Island Row', *Straits Times*, 25 January 2013.

50  Susumu Yabuki, 'Senkaku mondai no kosho keii no shinso', p. 1, http://www25.big.jp/~yabuki/2012/senkaku.pdf (revised edition of 28 September 2012), cited in Reinhard Drifte, *The Senkaku/Diaoyu Islands Territorial Dispute between Japan and China: Between the Materialization of the "China Threat" And Japan "Reversing The Outcome Of World War II"?*, UNISCI Discussion Papers no. 32 (Madrid: UNISCI, May 2013), p. 19, n. 57.

51  'China-watcher Yabuki says Senkakus are a Diplomatic Mistake by Japan', *Asahi Shimbun*, 12 December 2012.

52  James Przystup, John Bradford and James Manicom, 'Japan–China Maritime Confidence Building and Communications Mechanisms', *PacNet*, no. 67, 20 August 2013.

53  *Ibid.*

54  John Irish, 'Japan Urges "Hotline" With China, Plays Down Shrine Visit', Reuters, 9 January 2014.

55  *Ibid.*

56  Drifte, *The Senkaku/Diaoyu Islands Territorial Dispute*, pp. 29–30.

57  Interview in Tokyo, September 2013.

58  'Japan, China Navy Chiefs to Meet for Talks', *Japan Times*, 10 April 2014, http://www.japantimes.co.jp/news/2014/04/10/national/japans-top-naval-officer-tipped-for-talks-with-chinese-peer/#.Uo2UqfldWSo.

59  Jeremy Page, 'Pacific Navies Agree on Code of Conduct for Unplanned Encounters', *Wall Street Journal*, 22 April 2014, http://online.wsj.com/news/articles/SB10001424052702304049904579517342779110078.

60  Megha Rajagopalan, 'China Won't Swallow "Bitter Pill" of Ceding Sovereign Rights: Military Official', Reuters, 23 April 2014.

61  Wu Xinbo, 'America Should Step Back from the East China Sea Dispute', *New York Times*, 23 April 2014.

62  Taylor Fravel and Alastair Iain Johnston, 'Chinese Signaling in the East China Sea', *Washington Post*, 12 April 2014.

63  *Ibid.*

64  Pete Pedrozo, 'The U.S.–China Incidents at Sea Agreement: A Recipe for Disaster', *Journal of National Security Law & Policy*, vol. 6, no. 207, 7 March 2012, pp. 207–8.

65  See, for example, Kenneth N. Waltz, *Theory of International Politics* (New York: McGraw-Hill, 1979); Barry Buzan, 'Economic Structure and International Security: The Limits of the Liberal Case', *International Organization*, vol. 38, Autumn 1984, pp. 597–624; Dale C. Copeland, 'Economic Interdependence and War: A Theory of Trade Expectations', *International Security*, vol. 20, no. 4, Spring 1996, pp. 5–41.

66  Barbara W. Tuchman, *The March Of Folly: From Troy To Vietnam* (London: Abacus, 1985), p. 2.

# TABLES AND MAPS

Table 1: **Chinese Leaders, 1949–2014**

| Years | Premier | Years | President/Head of State | Years | 'Paramount Leader' |
|---|---|---|---|---|---|
| 1949–76 | Zhou Enlai | 1949–59 | Mao Zedong | 1949–76 | Mao Zedong |
| | | 1959–68 | Liu Shaoqi | | |
| | | 1968–72 | Song Qingling | | |
| | | 1968–75 | Dong Biwu | | |
| 1976–80 | Hua Guofeng | 1975–76 | Zhu De | 1976–78 | Hua Guofeng |
| | | 1976–78 | Song Qingling | | |
| | | 1978–83 | Ye Jianying | 1978–92 | Deng Xiaoping |
| 1980–88 | Zhao Ziyang | 1983–88 | Li Xiannian | | |
| 1988–98 | Li Peng | 1988–93 | Yang Shangkun | | |
| | | 1993–2003 | Jiang Zemin | 1992–2002 | Jiang Zemin |
| 1998–2003 | Zhu Rongji | | | | |
| 2003–13 | Wen Jiabao | 2003–13 | Hu Jintao | 2002–12 | Hu Jintao |
| 2013– | Li Keqiang | 2013– | Xi Jinping | 2012– | Xi Jinping |

Table 2: **Japanese Prime Ministers 1945–2014**

| Years | Prime Minister | Years | Prime Minister |
|---|---|---|---|
| 1945 | Naruhiko Higashikuni | 1989–91 | Toshiki Kaifu |
| 1945–46 | Kijuro Shidehara | 1991–93 | Kiichi Miyazawa |
| 1948–54 | Shigeru Yoshida | 1993–94 | Morihiro Hosokawa |
| 1954–56 | Ichiro Hatoyama | 1994 | Tsutomo Hata |
| 1956–57 | Tanzan Ishibashi | 1994–96 | Tomiichi Murayama |
| 1957–60 | Nobusuke Kishi | 1996–98 | Ryutaro Hashimoto |
| 1960–64 | Hayato Ikeda | 1998–2000 | Keizo Obuchi |
| 1964–72 | Eisaku Sato | 2000–01 | Yoshiro Mori |
| 1972–74 | Kakuei Tanaka | 2001–06 | Junichiro Koizumi |
| 1974–76 | Takeo Miki | 2006–07 | Shinzo Abe |
| 1976–78 | Takeo Fukuda | 2007–08 | Yasuo Fukuda |
| 1978–80 | Masayoshi Ohira | 2008–09 | Taro Aso |
| 1980–82 | Zenko Suzuki | 2009–10 | Yukio Hatoyama |
| 1982–87 | Yasuhiro Nakasone | 2010–11 | Naoto Kan |
| 1987–89 | Noboru Takeshita | 2011–12 | Yoshihiko Noda |
| 1989 | Sosuke Uno | 2012– | Shinzo Abe |

Table 3: **Chinese naval and air assets based near the Senkaku/Diaoyu Islands**

| | | |
|---|---|---|
| Submarines | 16 | |
| Principal Surface Combatants | 27 | 8 Destroyers, 19 Frigates |
| Bomber Aircraft | 48 | 12 PLANAF, 36 PLAAF |
| Tactical Aircraft | 400 | 100 PLANAF, 300 PLAAF |

| People's Liberation Army Navy Air Force (PLANAF) East Sea Fleet | |
|---|---|
| | ε12 bomber aircraft, ε100 tactical aircraft |
| 4th PLANAF Division | 2 Regiments with Su-30MK2 |
| 6th PLANAF Division | 3 Regiments with JH-7, H-6G, JH-7 |

| East Sea Fleet | |
|---|---|
| 22nd Submarine Flotilla (Daxie Dao) | 4 x *Yuan*-class, 4 x *Yuan* II-class |
| 42nd Submarine Flotilla (Xiangshan) | 8 x *Kilo*-class |
| 3rd Destroyer Flotilla (Dinghai) | 4 x *Sovremenny*-class, 2 x *Jiangkai* I-class, 2 x *Jiangkai* II-class |
| 6th Destroyer Flotilla (Dinghai) | 2 x *Luyang* II-class, 2 x *Luda* II-class, 4 x *Jiangwei* II-class, 2 x *Jiangkai* II-class |
| 3rd Frigate Squadron (Ningde) | 2 *Jianghu* V-class, 2 *Jiangwei* II-class, 1 *Jianghu* I-class (Fire Support Ship conversion) |
| 8th Frigate Squadron (Wusong) | 4 *Jiangwei* I-class |

| People's Liberation Army Air Force (PLAAF) Nanjing, Military Region Air Force (MRAF) | |
|---|---|
| | ε36 bomber ac, ε300 tactical ac |
| 3rd Fighter Division | 3 Regiments with J-7G, J-10/J-10A, Su-30MKK |
| 10th Bomber Division | 2 Regiments with H-6K, H-6H |
| 14th Fighter Division | 3 Regiments with J-11A, J-7E |
| 28th Attack Division | 3 Regiments with Q-5, JH-7A |
| Shanghai Base | 2 Brigades with J-7E/J-8H/JZ-8F/Su-30MKK |

Source: IISS

Table 4: **Japanese naval and air assets based near the Senkaku/Diaoyu Islands**

| Submarines | 0 | |
|---|---|---|
| Principal Surface Combatants | 16 | 12 Destroyers, 4 Destroyer Escorts |
| Bomber Aircraft | 20 | ε20 ASDF |
| Tactical Aircraft | 15 | ε15 MSDF |

| Naha Airbase | |
|---|---|
| JASDF | 204 Fighter Squadron (F-15J) - ε20 tactical aircraft |
| JMSDF | 5th Maritime Patrol Squadron (P-3C) - ε15 ASW aircraft |

| Sasebo Naval Base |
|---|
| 1 *Atago*-class cruiser (destroyer) |
| 2 *Asagiri*-class destroyers |
| 4 *Murasame*-class destroyers |
| 1 *Akizuki*-class destroyer |
| 1 *Hatakaze*-class destroyer |
| 2 *Kongou*-class destroyers |
| 1 *Shirane*-class destroyer |
| 1 *Abukuma*-class frigate (destroyer escort) |
| 3 *Hatsuyuki*-class frigates (destroyer escorts) |

Source: IISS

Map 1. **Japanese territorial incursions in China, 1895–1945**

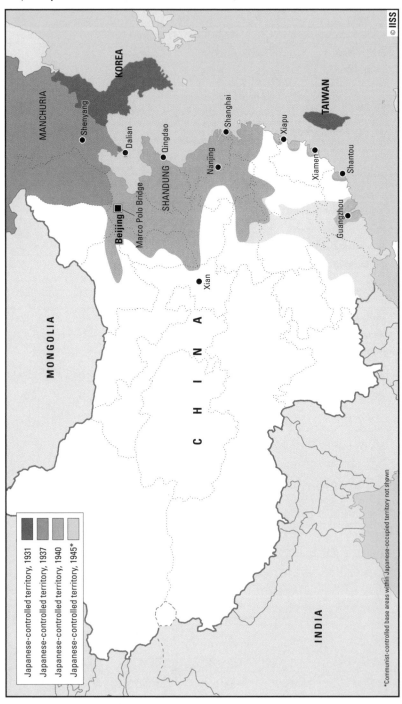

Map 2. **Northeast Asia and the Pacific**

Map 3. **The East China Sea**

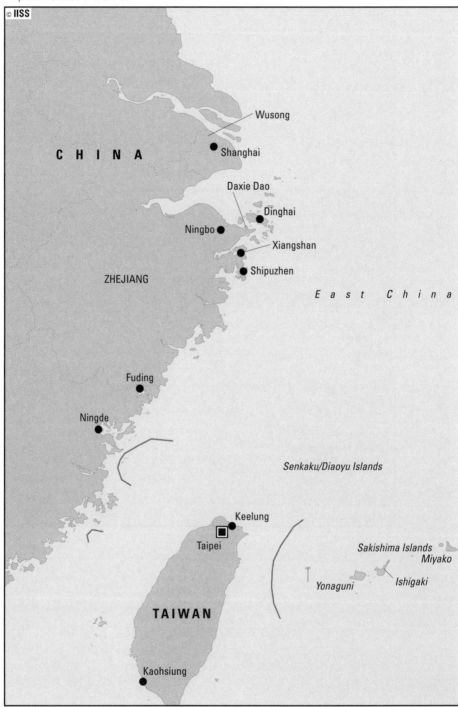

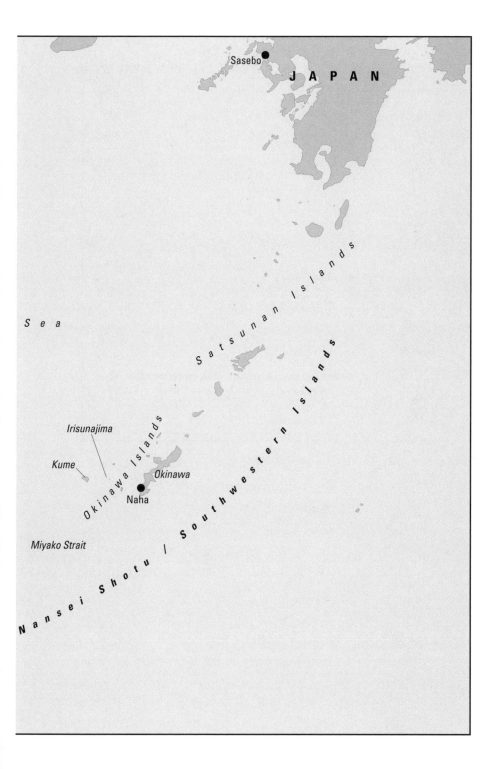

Map 4. **Chinese, Japanese and South Korean ADIZs and EEZs**

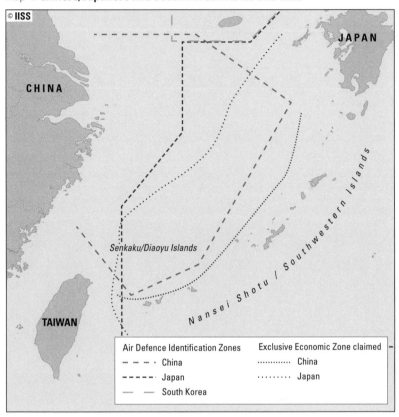

# INDEX

Adelphi books are published eight times a year by Routledge Journals, an imprint of Taylor & Francis, 4 Park Square, Milton Park, Abingdon, Oxfordshire OX14 4RN, UK.

A subscription to the institution print edition, ISSN 1944-5571, includes free access for any number of concurrent users across a local area network to the online edition, ISSN 1944-558X. Taylor & Francis has a flexible approach to subscriptions enabling us to match individual libraries' requirements. This journal is available via a traditional institutional subscription (either print with free online access, or online-only at a discount) or as part of the Strategic, Defence and Security Studies subject package or Strategic, Defence and Security Studies full text package. For more information on our sales packages please visit www.tandfonline.com/librarians_pricinginfo_journals.

| 2014 Annual Adelphi Subscription Rates | | | |
|---|---|---|---|
| Institution | £585 | $1,028 USD | €865 |
| Individual | £207 | $353 USD | €282 |
| Online only | £512 | $899 USD | €758 |

Dollar rates apply to subscribers outside Europe. Euro rates apply to all subscribers in Europe except the UK and the Republic of Ireland where the pound sterling price applies. All subscriptions are payable in advance and all rates include postage. Journals are sent by air to the USA, Canada, Mexico, India, Japan and Australasia. Subscriptions are entered on an annual basis, i.e. January to December. Payment may be made by sterling cheque, dollar cheque, international money order, National Giro, or credit card (Amex, Visa, Mastercard).

For a complete and up-to-date guide to Taylor & Francis journals and books publishing programmes, and details of advertising in our journals, visit our website: **http://www.tandfonline.com.**

Ordering information:
**USA/Canada:** Taylor & Francis Inc., Journals Department, 325 Chestnut Street, 8th Floor, Philadelphia, PA 19106, USA. **UK/Europe/Rest of World:** Routledge Journals, T&F Customer Services, T&F Informa UK Ltd., Sheepen Place, Colchester, Essex, CO3 3LP, UK.

Advertising enquiries to:
**USA/Canada**: The Advertising Manager, Taylor & Francis Inc., 325 Chestnut Street, 8th Floor, Philadelphia, PA 19106, USA. Tel: +1 (800) 354 1420. Fax: +1 (215) 625 2940. **UK/Europe/Rest of World**: The Advertising Manager, Routledge Journals, Taylor & Francis, 4 Park Square, Milton Park, Abingdon, Oxfordshire OX14 4RN, UK. Tel: +44 (0) 20 7017 6000. Fax: +44 (0) 20 7017 6336.

The print edition of this journal is printed on ANSI conforming acid-free paper by Bell & Bain, Glasgow, UK.